The M14-Type Rifle

A Shooter's and Collector's Guide

2nd Edition

Development History

Service Use

M21 Sniper Rifle

Custom Building M14-Type Rifles

Commercial Copies—Domestic/Chinese

National Match Rifles and Specifications

Operating Instructions

Cleaning and Maintenance Instructions

Trouble Shooting

National Match and Other Ammunition

Targeting and Shooting the M14-Type Rifle

Joe Poyer

North Cape Publications, Inc.

For **Kelsey, Kassie, Tyler and Kiley Marie**. May your Second Amendment rights still be respected when it is your turn to do a citizen's duty.

The author wishes to thank all those who helped in preparing this text, especially, Ken Fladrich, Mike Metzger and Woody Travis of the Armory of Orange, Orange, California; Jim Gronning and Randy Bimrose, Msgt, USMC (Ret.), Grúning Precision, Riverside, California; Clint Fowler, Custom Gunsmithing, Barboursville, Virginia; John Capalbo, Custom Gunsmithing, Garden Grove, California; Jack Friese, Armscorp, Inc., Baltimore, Maryland; Howard Chow, Entréprise Arms, Irwindale, California; Fred Johnson, USA (Ret.) and Brad Johnson.

This publication is designed to provide authoritative and accurate information of the subject matter covered. However, it should be recognized that serial numbers and dates, as well as other information given within are necessarily limited by the accuracy of source materials, the experimental nature of certain developments and procedures and the military nature of the basic rifle/ammunition system.

The M14-type rifle develops breech pressures in excess of 50,000 pounds per square inch. Use common sense at all times when shooting or working with an M14-type rifle.

Front cover: (l-r) Custom-built Entreprise M14A2 Rifle; Springfield Inc. M1A with ART II Telescopic Sight; Springfield National Armory M14A1.

Back cover: On the line: a properly turned-out shooter fires an M14 National Match Rifle.

ISBN 1-882391-18-7

North Cape Publications, **Inc.**, P.O. Box 1027, Tustin, California 92781
Phone **800 745-9714** for orders, **714 832-3621** for information. Fax **714 832-5302**
Email: **ncape@ix.netcom.com;** Internet web site: **http://www.northcapepubs.com**

Printed by KNI, Inc., Anaheim, CA 92806

Table of Contents

Receiver Markings of American-Made M14 and M14-type Rifles

U.S. Rifle
7.62 - MM M14
Springfield Armory
71223

Springfield
National Armory

U.S. Rifle
7.62 - MM M14
H.&.R Arms CO
432416

Harrington & Richardson

U.S. Rifle
7.62 - MM M14

TRW

1345085

Thompson, Ramo, Wooldrich

U.S. Rifle
7.62 - MM M14
Winchester
Trade Mark
148355

Olin Mathieson Corporation
(Winchester Division)

U.S. Rifle
7.62 - MM M1A
Springfield
Armory®
0314011

Springfield Armory

U.S. Rifle
7.62 - MM M14A2
Entreprise Arms
Irwindale, CA
ABNI

Entreprise Arms

U.S. Rifle
7.62 - MM M14 NM

A007007

Armscorp - National Match

U.S. Rifle
7.62 MM M14 NM
Smith Ent.
12543

Smith Enterprise

A.R. Sales Co.
So. El Monte, CA
Mark IV Cal. .308
0128

A.R. Sales Co.

M14 Rifle 7.62 x 51 mm NATO Caliber

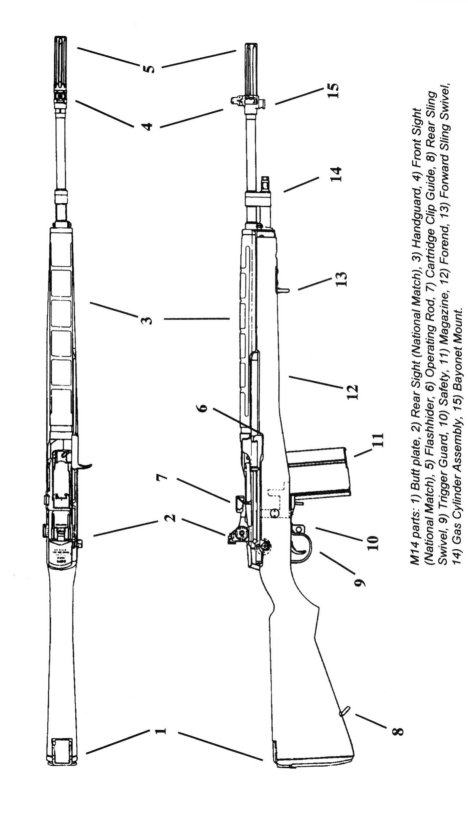

M14 parts: 1) Butt plate, 2) Rear Sight (National Match), 3) Handguard, 4) Front Sight (National Match), 5) Flashhider, 6) Operating Rod, 7) Cartridge Clip Guide, 8) Rear Sling Swivel, 9) Trigger Guard, 10) Safety, 11) Magazine, 12) Forend, 13) Forward Sling Swivel, 14) Gas Cylinder Assembly, 15) Bayonet Mount.

FOREWORD

The M14-Type rifle has established a niche in the heart of many American high power shooters. Few other rifles are so susceptible to the attentions of an experienced gunsmith and a disciplined shooter. At every high power match in the country, you will see a wide variety of M14-type rifles from actual M14s in the hands of military personnel to one of the many production or custom-built civilian M14-types described in the following pages.

There are few books available on the M14 and fewer still on the M14-type rifles as a glance at the Bibliography in Appendix G will attest. And those that do exist concentrate on either the history of the rifle's development or how to shoot and customize it. In this book, we are attempting to do both, as well as provide the collector with information regarding this ultimate expression of John C. Garand's genius. While the military M14 is not available to collectors as is the M1 Garand, the Model 1903 Springfield and a host of other and earlier military firearms, there are sufficient parts on the market to enable collectors to assemble near military-correct rifles on semiautomatic receivers — with due regard for the provisions of the 1994 Crime Control Act which are outlined in Appendix F.

But it was the earlier 1968 Gun Control Act which dismayed many match and precision shooters, as well as collectors, because it made it all but impossible to own an M14 rifle. The 1968 Gun Control act stated that if a military firearm was designed and produced as a select fire weapon, it was classified as a machine gun and therefore, could not be sold to civilian shooters, not even through the Director of Civilian Marksmanship (DCM). Another instance of legislative and bureaucratic expediency over the rights of law abiding citizens, courtesy of the United States Congress.

It apparently was never noted with sufficient impact to impress itself on the minds of legislators that in the more than sixty years of history to that point, the number of times a DCM-supplied firearm was used to commit a crime was so low that not even that accumulator of data on American citizens — law-abiding as well as non-law-abiding — the Federal Bureau of Investigation, had ever entertained the idea of gathering such statistics.

So for several years after the M14 became the National Match rifle, civilian shooters were handicapped in matches against military personnel. Handicapped that is until the market moved and brought forth a civilian, semiautomatic version of the M14. Now, almost thirty years later, lazy, inept and dishonest legislators in the federal Congress and many state legislatures are again gathering forces to eliminate semiautomatic rifles and further restrict your right to own and use a variety of other firearms without regard to the constitutionally guaranteed rights of American citizens.

So, if you wish to continue to enjoy building, shooting and collecting the M14-type rifle — and other firearms as well — then you must help stop those elitist legislators and their allies, who are to arrogant, uncaring, lazy or inept to study and consider the effects of such bills on law-abiding citizens. And they can be stopped, but only if all honest, law-abiding citizens organize and make certain that they do not succeed. Use your voice to set the record straight wherever possible, and use your vote to chase them from office. The author wishes to take this opportunity to urge you to join, or rejoin, the National Rifle Association. If you love firearms and wish to retain your right to own and shoot them, you must make your voice heard and the NRA is the best way to do so.

Finally, I would like to thank gunsmiths Ken Fladrich, Fred Johnson, Jim Gronning and Randy Bimrose for their consultation and advice. If, in spite of their diligent efforts, errors have crept into the manuscript, then the fault is entirely mine.

Joe Poyer

Conventions

The M14 was, and refers to, a select fire military rifle. The M1A is a semiautomatic rifle produced by Springfield, Inc., a commercial company and not the former National Armory at Springfield, MA. The name, "M1A" is a registered trademark and applies only to that company's products.

In this text, all commercial, semiautomatic copies of the M14 are referred to either by their trademarked names, or generically, as M14-type rifles.

Any information presented in these pages regarding the select fire characteristics of the M14 rifle is included either in a historical context or for clarification.

Markings originally stamped or engraved on the rifle, or its parts by the manufacturer are enclosed in quotations. The quotations are not part of the marking, unless so stated.

All directions are given from the shooter's point of view, i.e., looking toward the muzzle.

The reader will find information repeated throughout the text. This was done deliberately to save having to search back and forth to find a specific bit of information.

1: THE M14 RIFLE

It was the shortest lived combat rifle in the history of the United States Army. In fact, it has proven far more popular with civilian match shooters than with the soldiers who trained with and carried it for such a short time. Today, it survives in military service in the form of a sniper rifle (reserve) and line-launcher for the U.S. Navy. The M14 was a rifle (Figure 1-1) whose time had come ten years before, and passed even as it was adopted. It was a good combat rifle, but not a great rifle. It was too heavy and cumbersome for the task for which it was designed. It's ammunition was too bulky and far too powerful for the modern battlefield and its breakage rate was far too high. Even so, a hard core of combat infantrymen and Marines loved the M14 and protested loudly at its passing. And civilian high-power competition shooters not only love the M14, but swear by it for accuracy and range.

The M14 was a product of the U.S. Army's Ordnance Engineers who had worked such miracles during World War II keeping the American military and many of our Allies supplied with weapons and ammunition. Beginning in the summer of 1945 when an invasion of the Japanese home islands was imminent and the horrors of the Philippine, Iwo Jima and Okinawa campaigns were underway, development of a new selective fire combat rifle began.

John Garand's M1 rifle was the starting point and by the end of August in 1945, the new rifle, designated the T20E2 (T for test) was ready. But the atomic bomb abruptly ended World War II. Millions of lives on all sides were spared and the world struggled to recover from the most costly and vicious war in human history. The development of the new rifle was relegated to the back burner.

Over the next decade, Ordnance officials struggled to keep the new selective fire combat rifle alive. Fresh in their minds were the lessons learned in Europe, Africa and the Pacific. The M1 Garand and the Soviet's SVT38/40 semiautomatic rifle had proven the superiority of massed, rapid small arms fire. Toward the end of the war, the German 7.92 Machine Pistol 43, or as it is more popularly known, the *Sturmgehwere 44*, the predecessor of all modern assault rifles, astonished the Allies in the Ardennes and along the hard road to Berlin with its superiority over semiautomatic rifles. The American combat infantryman would be at a distinct disadvantage, they realized in the next conflict without a selective fire weapon. And the Korean Conflict proved them right.

Following a series of development trials culminating in a rifle design designated the T44, the new selective fire rifle was accepted. On May 1, 1957, it was standarized as the M14 rifle.

But the new combat rifle was to be short-lived. Production did not begin until 1958 and deliveries not until mid-1959. But already, the new rifle was obsolete. It was heavy and even with the reduced size and weight of the new 7.62 x 51 mm NATO cartridge, the ammunition was to heavy for the quantities that the modern infantryman needed to carry. And the parts breakage problem persisted, in spite of everything ordnance engineers and designers could do. The cartridge was

Fig. 1-1. The M14 Rifle system consisted of the basic select fire rifle, bipod, magazine, M6 Bayonet and sling. The bipod was issued only to those rifles designated as "Squad Automatic Weapons" (SAW).

The M14 Rifle: Bottom to Top, M14A1, National Armory at Springfield; M1A, Springfield Inc.; M14-Type Long Range Match Rifle custom built by Grüning Precision, Riverside, California. Author's collection.

Fig. 1-2. A Ninth Army soldier fires his M1 Garand at retreating Nazis during street fighting in Cologne, 6 March 1945. US Army Photo

simply to powerful for a selective fire weapon that could be carried by the individual infantryman. By 1965, the M14 was declared obsolete and replaced by the M16 rifle in the new NATO caliber of 5.56 x 45 mm.

The M14 had not even been fully issued in the U.S. Army and Marine Corps when it was abruptly withdrawn from service. But as short-lived as it was, the M14 had, and continues to exert, a profound influence on civilian shooters, particularly in rifle matches at all ranges. The M14 may not have proven serviceable to the military, but it has certainly found a place in the affections of match rifle shooters in the United States, both in civilian and military life. So much so that numerous civilian versions of the rifle have been developed and sold in the United States since the late 1960s.

For a complete history of the development and service life of the M14 rifle and the rise of civilian versions, please see Appendix A and Chapter 5, The Civilian M14s.

Fig. 1-3. The M14 remains in service nearly twenty years after it was officially replaced. This Navy SEAL, participating in the maritime interdiction operation in the Persian Gulf after Operation Desert Storm, prepares his M14 rifle. Note that a pistol grip has been added to the forearm and an Aimpoint sighting device has been mounted in place of a telescopic sight. Photo by PH2 Milton R. Savage, US Navy.

Fig. 1-4. The M14 today is widely used as a sniper rifle in either its M21 guise or as a M14-type commercial rifle as that being fired here on the range by a police sniper.

2: M14 RIFLE: BASIC DESCRIPTION AND DATA

A detailed description of the M14 rifle will help to acquaint both the new owner and the experienced shooter with the rifle. Excepting only the paragraphs dealing with the full automatic features of the military M14 rifle, the following description also applies to civilian versions of the M14, sometimes known as the M1A®. It should be noted that the term M1A® is a registered trademark and is properly applied only to those rifles manufactured by the commercial company, Springfield, Inc. At the end of this section, every part of the M14 is listed complete with its "Drawing Number" which also serves as its inventory and part number. In many instances, this number is also stamped on the part.

Rifle

The 7.62-mm rifle M14 is a light weight, air cooled, gas operated, magazine fed, shoulder weapon, designed primarily for semiautomatic or full automatic fire at the cyclic rate of 750 rounds per minute (Figure 2-1). The rifle is chambered for the 7.62 mm NATO cartridge and is designed to accommodate a 20-round cartridge magazine, the rifle bipod M2, grenade launcher M76, and the bayonet knife M6. The grenade launcher sight M15 is also installed when the grenade launcher is used. For training purposes, a blank ammunition firing attachment M12 and breech shield M3 are used and during cold weather or Arctic operations the winter trigger kit is also utilized.

Fig. 2-1. The M14 is an air-cooled, gas operated, magazine fed select fire rifle.

Sling

Two types of slings were used with the M14 rifle. The most common was the canvas or nylon M1 Sling. The sling was issued in two lengths: the earliest was 46 inches long and used a single snap-on hook and a buckle sewn onto one end (Figure 2-2). The later sling was 64.5 inches long and had a single buckle sewn onto one end and used two snap-on hooks. This longer sling was used with the M14E2 which was intended for use as a squad automatic weapon. Both slings were 1.28 inches wide

and dyed green drab. The buckle was 1.5 inches wide and the hooks are 1.15 inches wide. The snap on caps or hooks and the buckle were steel, parkerized black, although some made in the 1950s have blackened brass hardware.

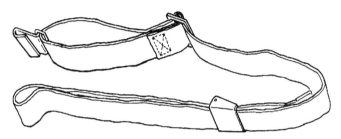

Fig. 2-2. The issue sling for the M14 was the M1, Type 4 made of canvas or nylon. The Model 1907 leather sling was also used.

Magazine

The magazine was made of sheet steel and parkerized black (Figure 2-3). It held 20 rounds of 7.62 x 51 NATO ammunition. It was 6 inches high by 2.9 inches deep and 0.98 inches wide. The magazine was an assembly consisting of the sheet steel body, a sheet steel follower, a sheet steel removable bottom for cleaning and a spring that drove the follower.

Magazine Pouches

Two types of magazine pouches were issued with the M14 rifle. Both were designed to be worn on the belt, both were made of woven canvas or nylon and both were dyed green drab. The first was a single pocket pouch measuring 11 inches long (opened flat) by 3.8 inches wide at the rear by 1.25 inches deep (Figure 2-4). The pouch was mounted on a single piece of canvas 23 inches long that was doubled and sewn to form a belt loop at the back with a cover that folded over the top of the pouch. The pouch body was 5.3 inches long by 3.3 inches wide and 1.1

Fig. 2-3. M14 magazines were made of sheet steel and each held 20 rounds of 7.62 mm NATO ammunition.

inches deep. A snap fastened the cover closed and two grommets were sewn into the bottom corners.

The second type of pouch held two M14 magazines. It was 6 inches high by 4.3 inches wide by 2.4 inches deep (Figure 2-5). It was designated "Pouch, Small Arms, Ammunition, Universal." It was designed to be fastened to a cartridge belt by ALICE clips.

Fig. 2-4. M1961 Magazine Pouch issued by the USMC for the M14 magazine.

Fig. 2-5. M1956 Pouch, Small Arms, Universal magazine pouch issued for the M14 by the U.S. Army. Also used for M1 Carbine magazines.

Bipod

The rifle bipod M2 is a folding mount which clamps onto the gas cylinder and gas cylinder lock of the rifle (Figure 2-6). It is composed of three main groups: the yoke assembly and the right and left leg assemblies. A self-locking bolt locks the jaws of the yoke assembly when clamped on the rifle. The bipod legs can be folded back along side the forend. They can be extended by depressing the catch on each leg. The bipod

Fig. 2-6. The M2 bipod for the M14A1 rifle.

mount allows the rifle to be rotated left or right to compensate for uneven ground.

Grenade Launcher M76

The launcher is utilized for launching grenades from the rifle. The launcher slides over the flash suppressor and is secured to the rifle by a clip latch that snaps over the bayonet lug of the flash suppressor (Figure 2-7).

Fig. 2-7. M76 Grenade Launcher.

Grenade Launcher Sight Ml5

The sight is used with the grenade launcher. It consists of the mounting scale plate and sight bar assembly (Figure 2-8). The mounting scale plate is attached to the

Fig. 2-8. M15 Grenade Launching Sight

left side of the stock by two screws. The sight bar assembly attaches to the mounting plate.

Bayonet-Knife M6 and Bayonet-Knife Scabbard M8Al

The bayonet knife is designed for use on the rifle in close combat (Figure 2-9). It connects to the bayonet lug of the flash suppressor and a ring on the guard which encircles the flash suppressor. The bayonet-knife scabbard is made of fiberglass

Fig. 2-9. M6 Bayonet and M8A1 Scabbard.

and when the bayonet is not mounted on the rifle, it is carried on the belt in the scabbard. The scabbard used was the M8A1, first developed during World War II for the M1 Carbine's M4 bayonet.

Blank Ammunition Firing Attachment M12 and Breech Shield M3

The blank ammunition firing attachment is used only during training to fire blank cartridges (Figure 2-10). The attachment contains an orifice tube which slides into the muzzle opening of the flash suppressor and is secured to the bayonet lug by a spring clip latch. The breech shield is used with the blank adaptor only to fire blank cartridges. The breech shield connects to the cartridge guide on the receiver and is secured within the guide by a

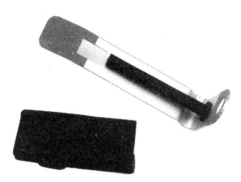

Fig. 2-10. M12 Blank Firing Attachment for the M14 Rifle.

spring plunger. The breech shield protects the shooter by deflecting empty cartridge cases during ejection.

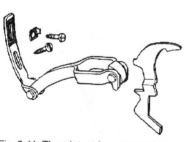

Fig. 2-11. The winter trigger assembly was developed for use in Arctic conditions.

Winter Trigger Kit

The winter trigger kit is used during cold or Arctic operations. It consists of a winter safety and winter trigger assembly and is secured to the bottom portion of the stock (Figure 2-12).

Table 1
M14 Rifle And Accessories Data Tables
Rifle

Weight of basic rifle with equipment and empty magazine	9.1 lb (approx.
Weight of basic rifle with equipment ready to fire, fully loaded magazine	11.0 lb
Length of rifle with flash suppressor	44.3 in.
Length of barrel	22.0 in.
Type of firing	Rotating bolt
Method of actuation	Gas operation
Cyclic rate	750 rd per min
Cooling	Air
Muzzle velocity	2,800 fps
Magazine Capacity	20 rd
Ammunition types	NATO 7.62 mm ball, AP, tracer, dummy and blank

Sling

Length	46 or 64.5 in.
Width	1.28 in

Magazine Pouches

	Single	
Double Length	11 in	6 in
Width	3.8 in	4.3 in
Depth	1.25 in	2.4 in
Capacity	1-20	2-20

Bipod

Weight	1-3/4 lb
Height	
Legs in closed position	9-3/4 in.
Legs in extended position	13 in.
Length	
legs folded for transportation	11-3/4 in.
Spread of leg assemblies	
Closed position	15-1/4 in.(approx)
Extended position	19-3/4 in.

Grenade Launcher M76 and Grenade Launcher Sight M15

Grenade launcher	
Length Overall	8-1/4 in.
Weight	7 oz
Grenade launcher sight	
Length overall	5- 1/4 in.
Weight	5 oz

Bayonet-Knife M6

Length overall	11 1/4 in.
Weight	12 oz
Blade length	6-5/8 in.
Width	7/8 in.

Bayonet-Knife Scabbard M8AI

Length	14 in
Width	2-3/8 in.

Blank Ammunition Firing Attachment M12

Length overall	5-1/4 in.
Weight	2-3/4 oz
Width	1 in.

Breech Shield M3

Length overall	3-3/8 in.
Weight	1 1/4 oz
Width	1-1/4 in.

Winter Trigger

Length overall	4-1/8 in.
Weight	2-1/2 oz
Width	3/4 in.

Winter Safety

Length overall	3-1/4 in.
Weight	1 1/2 oz
Width	1-3/8 in.

M14 Parts and their Identification

Each part of the M14 was assigned an engineering drawing number. This system had two advantages. First, it provided a specific set of standards for each part to meet, thus insuring both quality and complete interchangeablity, as well as making certain that only the latest authorized drawing was in use. Secondly, it served as a "parts identification system" within the huge supply system of the federal government. For the civilian shooter interested in using only U.S. government contractor - built parts, an understanding of the part number and contractor's code procedures are essential.

Until the end of the Korean War, the actual drawing number served as the part number and was marked on all major parts. In the early 1950s, the new Federal Stock Number system was developed and employed 11 digits. Drawing numbers were incorporated directly into that system by attaching a prefix. This system in turn was superceded by the National Stock Number system, but still the drawing number remained incorporated into the identifying number assigned to each part.

Most M14 parts are identified by a seven digit number beginning with 1, 5, 6 or 7. Five parts are identified with an eight digit number. In all, sixty-six parts for the M14 are listed in inventory.

Table 2
M14 — Standard Nomenclature

Aperture	6008868
Aperture (National Match 0.0595)	7791133
Aperture (National Match 0.0520)	7781282
Band, Front	7267001
Band, Hand Guard	6008870
Band (standard — chrome lined)	7790190
Band (National Match)	7791362
Base, Rear Sight (standard)	5546001
Base, Rear Sight (National Match)	7791571
Bolt	7790186
Cover, Rear Sight	6008872
Cylinder, Gas	7790902
Ejector, Cartridge with Spring	7267015
Extractor, Cartridge	7791578
Ferrule, Stock	7267017
Guard, Assembly Hand, Fiber Glass	7791286
Guard, Trigger	7790990
Guide, Cartridge Clip	7790184
Guide, Operating Rod	7267025
Guide, Operating Rod Spring	7267027
Hammer	5546008
Housing, Hammer Spring	6008883
Housing, Trigger	7267030
Knob, Windage, Rear Sight, (standard)	7312737
Knob, Windage, Rear Sight (National Match)	7790386
Latch, Magazine	7267032
Lock, Bolt	7267034
Lock, Gas Cylinder	7790188
Magazine, Cartridge (20 rounds)	7790183
Nut, Flash Suppressor	7267039
Nut, Square (for plastic stock)	7791339
Pin, Bolt Lock	None
Pin, Firing (chrome plated)	11686413
Pin, Firing (not chrome plated)	None
Pin, Hammer	5013668
Pin, Magazine Latch	7791418
Pin, Trigger	7791367
Pinion Assembly, Rear Sight Elevating	11010363
Piston, Gas	7267047
Plate Assembly, Butt, Hinged	7790686
Plug, Gas Cylinder	7267053
Plunger, Extractor Spring	6008618
Plunger, Hammer Spring	6008880
Receiver	7790789
Retainer, Bolt Roller	7267059
Retainer, Nut and Bolt (for plastic stock)	11010414
Rod, Operating	7267064
Roller, Bolt	7267065
Safety	5546015
Screw, Butt Plate (for plastic stock)	7791267
Screw, Butt Plate (for wood stock)	7791036
Screw, Butt Plate, Long	6008881
Screw, Cap, Socket Head (Front Sight)	11010298
Screw, Set, Hex, Socket	7790300
Sight, Front (standard)	7791445
Sight, Front (National Match 0.062)	7791122
Spindle, Valve	7267604
Spring, Bolt Lock	None
Spring, Hammer	6008887
Spring, Magazine Latch	7267041
Spring, Operating Rod	7267079
Spring, Safety	7267080
Spring, Spindle Valve	7267605
Stock, Subassembly (standard wood)	7790810
Stock, Subassembly (standard plastic)	11686427
Stock, Subassembly (National Match)	11010262

Suppressor, Flash	7791053
Swivel, Butt Stock	6008889
Trigger and Sear Assembly	7267090

All M14 parts were referenced by "drawing numbers" plus a manufacturer identifier stamped on all major parts.

Fig. 2-12. Springfield National Arsenal identifier.

Springfield-made parts were marked "SA" followed by the drawing number, except for safeties which were marked only "SA" (Figure 2-12). Harrington & Richardson stamped all major parts "HRA," including rear sight bases which were marked "H&R" or "HR," bolts marked "HR" or "HR-N" and trigger housings were marked "HRA" or "HR-N" (Figure 2-13). Barrel bands were stamped "HR" on the inside.

Winchester major parts were stamped with their drawing number and the Winchester code, "66118" (Figure 2-14). Early trigger housings were marked "WRA," later ones "OM" for Olin Mathieson, Winchester's parent company at that time. Safteies were marked "K-8" or "OM." Other markings observed on safeties

Fig. 2-13. Harrington & Richardson identifier

were "H" and "F," on the right side so that the marking was visible when assembled. These initials are believed to be inspector's approval markings. Rear sight bases were marked "OM" and elevation knobs were usually marked "WC E" and windage knobs, "SWK." Barrels were marked with the Winchester proof mark, the W/P inside an oval (Figure 2-15).

Fig. 2-14. Winchester identifier.

TRW manufactured only eleven components themselves, farming the rest out to subconctractors. They made barrels, bolts, connections, flash suppressors, gas cylinders, hammers, operating rods, pistons, rear sight bases, receivers and trigger hous-

ings. All were marked "TRW" (Figure 2-16).

Numerous subcontractors also manufactured various parts, but a complete listing is beyond the scope of this book. Two major subcontractors, however, deserve attention as the spare parts they manufactured are sought after.

Fig. 2-15. Winchester logotype as marked on M14 barrels.

Saco-Lowell Division of Maremont Corporation manufactured barrels, operating rods, gas cylinders, gas pistons and other unmarked parts as a contractor to both Springfield and Harrington & Richardson. Saco parts were marked "SAK."

The Canadian Arsenal, Ltd of Mississauga, Ontario (Long Branch) manufactured National Match barrels under a contract extended by the Ordnance Department. These extremely fine barrels can be identified by "CA" code on the barrel (Figure 2-17). They are also engraved, "NM" for National Match behind the flash suppressor mounting.

Fig. 2-16. Thompson Ramo Woolridge (TRW) identifier.

CA7791362 4 67C8549

Fig. 2-17. Canadian Arsenals, Ltd. National Match barrel identifier.

M14 magazine codes observed to date include "HR-R" (Harrington & Richardson), "W" (Winchester), "C.M.I.," "R," "BRW/S1," "BR-W/B2," "BRW/S-1," "OM" (Olin Mathieson), "KMT Co," "UHC" and "AM"(Figure 2-18).

Fig. 2-18. M14 magazine manufacturer's marking.

Manufacturer's codes, as well as the part number, are stamped on certain more important parts. The manufacturer's codes, or identifiers, are listed in Table 3, in bold type.

Table 3
Parts Markings

Part	Manufacturer	Markings*
Bolt	Springfield National Armory	Part #, Heat Treatment Lot, **SA****
	Winchester	Part #, Heat Treatment Lot, **66118**
	Harrington & Richardson	Part #, Heat Treatment Lot, **HRA, HRT & HRL, HR-N**
	TRW	Part #, Heat Treatment Lot, **TRW**
Barrel	Springfield National Armory	Part #, **SA**
	Winchester	Company Name, Part #, **Winchester Logo**
	Harrington & Richardson	Part #, **HRA**
	TRW	Part #, **TRW**
	Canadian Arsenals	"CA" part number, NM (behind flash suppressor)
	SACO	**SAK**
Trigger Guard	Springfield	Part #, **SA**
	Winchester	Part #, **66118**
	Harrington & Richardson	Part #, **HRA**
	TRW	Part #, **TRW**
Hammer	Springfield	Part #, **SA**
	Winchester	Part #, **66118** (also **OM**)
	Harrington & Richardson	Part #, **HRA** or **H&R**
	TRW	Part #, **TRW**
Safety	Springfield	Part #, **SA**
	Winchester	Part #, **66118** (also **OM**)
	Harrington & Richardson	Part #, **HRA**
Magazine	"**HR-R**" (Harrington & Richardson), "**W**" (Winchester), "**C.M.I.**," "**R**," "**BRW/S1**," "**BR-W/B2**," "**BRW/S-1**," "**OM**" (Olin Mathieson), "**KMT Co,**" and "**UHC.**"	

*   Inspector's markings will often be found on M14 parts. These may consist of one or two alphabetical characters or numbers.

** SA = Springfield National Armory; W, OM, 66118 = Winchester; HRA, HR-A = Harrington & Richardson and TRW = Thompson Ramo Woolridge.

3: THE NATIONAL MATCH M14

This section describes the National Match M14 and illustrates how it differed from the standard M14 in general terms. For National Match rifle specifications as established by the U.S. Army, please refer to Appendix B.

In 1962, the M14 was designated the National Match Rifle, replacing the M1 Garand. As expected, the changeover took some time, especially among civilian participants who were convinced that their M1 Garand National Match rifles were far superior. A total of 18,325 M14 National Match rifles were manufactured by the U.S. Army (Table 4) — but not including USMC, Navy or Air Force National Match M14s. Note that *new* rifles were manufactured as National Match rifles until 1964, afterward, existing M14 rifles were rebuilt as production had ended.

the axis of the stock. Straight-grained wood was required for strength, so no national match stock will show significant "figure" or grain. The walnut from which the stocks were made

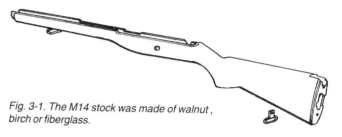

Fig. 3-1. The M14 stock was made of walnut , birch or fiberglass.

was very close-grained. National Match stocks are usually a few ounces heavier than standard G.I. stocks (Figure 3-1)

Table 4
M14 National Match Rifle Production
1962-1967

Year	By	New/ Rebuilt	Annual Total	Cummulative Totals
1962	Springfield	N	3,000	3,000
1963	Springfield	N	3,500	6,500
1964	TRW	N	4874	11,374
1965	Springfield	R*	2,094	13,468
1966	Springfield	R	2,395	15,863
1967	Rock Island Arsenal	R	2,462	18,325

* Rebuilt service rifles. M14 Production ended in 1964

The argument over which rifle was more accurate, the M1 Garand or the M14, raged for several years following the adoption of the M14. The Army Material Command was ordered to improve the accuracy of the M14 and over a several year period, the following procedures were adopted. The same argument would rage twenty years later between the M14 and the M16A2 rifles.

Stock

The stock was made of American walnut and was specified as solid heartwood with the direction of the grain parallel with

Fig. 3-2. Proof applied to all US military rifles between 1873 and 1966.

The forward part of the wrist on all stocks mounted to rifles and proof-tested was marked with the firing proof "P" which was 5/16 inches high and enclosed within a 1/2 inch diameter circle (Figure 3-2). The Department of Defense Final Inspection stamp — an Eagle clutching three arrows contained in a box with rounded corners 1/2 inch high — was stamped on the left side of the stock below the rear of the receiver (Figure 3-3).

Fig. 3-3. Defense eagle acceptance stamp used from Autumn 1953 to the end of M14 production in 1966.

The barrel channel received additional inletting to make certain that the barrel never came in contact with the stock, nor with the handguard.

The receiver, stock liner and the trigger housing assembly were individually fitted to the stock and bedded in place with a fiberglass compound. A clearance was left between the rear of the receiver bedding surface and the receiver rail bedding surfaces. The rear legs of the receiver were required to bear evenly on the recoil shoulders of the stock liner. To identify the components, the stock and trigger housing were inscribed with the last four digits of the receiver's serial number.

Finally, the stock was finished with tung oil (also known as China oil) which sealed the wood grain and prevented absorption of moisture from the atmosphere which could cause the wood to swell and interfere with accuracy.

Butt Plate

The standard M14 buttplate was seated on the butt end of the stock (Figure 3-4). The metal of the buttplate could not overlap the wood, i.e., the wood must be "proud" of the metal.

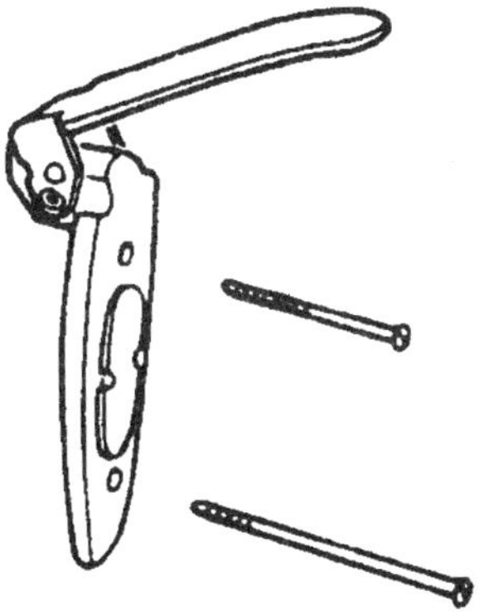

Stock Ferrule

The stock ferrule was allowed to press against the top part of the front band but not the lower part. The minimum clearance allowed between the stock ferrule and the front band was 1/64 inch (Figure 3-5).

Fig. 3-5. M14 Stock ferrule.

Fig. 3-4. M14 Buttplate.

Hand Guard

The hand guard (Figure 3-6) was not allowed to contact the stock. The lower edges were relieved as necessary.

Barrel

The barrel was specially straightened to a specific tolerance which required that the bore not deviate more than 0°2' 23" from the centerline. The measurement was made with a self-aligning expansion plug. The muzzle was crowned concentric to the bore at a 90 degree angle and deburred.

The letters "NM" for National Match 1/8 inch high were engraved on the top of the barrel midway between the front hand guard and the front sight. To show that the National Match barrel had been proof fired, the proof letter "P" was prick punched in the upper loop. Bore diameter was 0.300 + 0.001 and groove diameter was 0.3075 + 0.0010. Barrel head space was 1.6355 to 1.6385 inches (Figure 3-7).

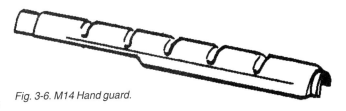

Fig. 3-6. M14 Hand guard.

Barrel Bore Diameter: The Arsenal used air gages to accurately measure and control bore diameters of the National Match rifle. A constant flow of air passed through the gage and out through orifices in the spindles. If the bore diameter was restricted, the air flow was reduced and the float rode higher in the air column. If the bore was overlarge, more air escaped, the pressure fell and the float dropped. As the spindle traversed the barrel, readings were taken at a number of points, thus checking the uniformity of the barrel land and groove diam-

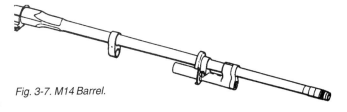

Fig. 3-7. M14 Barrel.

eters from end to end. The air gage permitted measurements of diameters to an accuracy of 0.0001 inch variation.

Bores which were within dimensional limits, but tapered slightly from the breech to the muzzle end, were passed. But a bore which was larger at the muzzle than at the breech was rejected. The last four inches at the muzzle were held to particularly close tolerances.

Barrel Straightness: Lack of barrel straightness was a major cause of targeting rejects because the groups were too far off from the sight setting. But in relation to accuracy, or the ability of weapon to place shots consistently within a given area without regard to sight alignment, barrel straightness was not considered to be as important.

The Arsenal developed an optical instrument for determining straightness within 0.0002 slope units of angular movement, or 42 seconds. The instrument moved a mirrored plug through the barrel bore by means of a handwheel. The image of the reticle was reflected through a prism system to a screen.

11

Each barrel was checked for straightness using this instrument. National Match barrels had to show no deviation greater than 0 degrees, 2 minutes, 23 seconds.

Proof Firing: Each barrel was subjected to proof firing prior to assembly to the receiver. The barrel had to withstand one high pressure test cartridge (approximately 70,000 pounds per square inch) without evidence of failure as determined by magnetic particle inspection.

Each completed weapon was proof fired with one round of high pressure test ammunition. After firing, the weapon was carefully inspected for evidence of failure. The spent proof-cartridge case was closely examined for bulges, splits, rings or any evidence of other defects. Any defects found caused the rifle to be rejected.

Fig. 3-8. A punch prick was made inside the "P" proof mark on the M14 barrel.

Immediately after proof firing the prescribed proof marks (Figure 3-8) were be placed on each acceptable barrel, bolt, stock and receiver.

Front Sight

The rear edge of the National Match front sight blade was 0.065 ± .005 inches wide. The top of the front sight blade was square with the sides and all edges and corners could not exceed 0.003 inch radius, producing sharp edges. The front sight (Figure 3-9) was

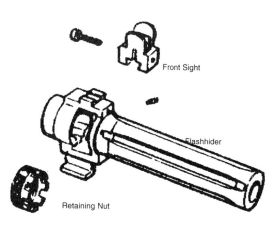

Fig. 3-9. M14 Front sight and flash suppressor assembly.

not allowed to hang over the sides of the gas cylinder. The National Match front sight blade was identified with the letters "NM" and the number "0.062" marked on the right side.

Gas Cylinder Assembly

Gas cylinders for the National Match rifle were selected to fit tightly enough on the barrel and splines so that it no rotational movement was evident (Figure 3-10). The gas cylinder lock was hand-tightened against the shoulder on the barrel so that it stopped slightly beyond the 6 o'clock position, but not in excess of 8 o'clock. The gas cylinder lock

Fig. 3-10. M14 Gas cylinder Assembly.

was then backed off just enough to align with the gas cylinder at the 6 o'clock position. The gas cylinder was then moved forward against the gas cylinder lock and the gas cylinder lock screw or plug was tightened down to 15 foot pounds ± 2 pounds.

Flash Suppressor

The flash suppressor was screwed on to the barrel and secured by the flash suppressor nut (refer to Figure 3-9). A set screw held the flash suppressor nut in place. No rotational or longitudinal movement was allowed when pressure was applied by hand. To test the flash suppressor, a plug with a lower diameter of 0.2993 inches 2.5 inches long and an upper diameter of 0.329 inches was inserted into the flash suppressor after it was attached to the barrel. The narrow diameter of the plug had to enter the bore freely for 2.5 inches without any contact or binding against the interior of the flash suppressor.

Receiver

The selector shaft assembly enabling full automatic fire was removed and the selector shaft mount was welded over. The rear legs of the receiver were modified so that they bore equally on the recoil shoulders of the stock liner. The initials "NM" were engraved on the National Match receiver. And the left side of the breech ring was prick punched after proof firing (Figure 3-11).

Fig. 3-11. M14 receiver.

Bolt

A standard M14 bolt was used (Figure 3-12). It had to headspace between 1.6335 and 1.6385 inches. It was prick punched on the top of the bolt after proof firing.

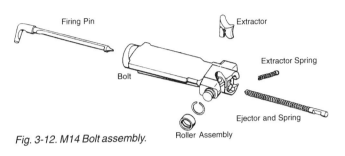

Fig. 3-12. M14 Bolt assembly.

Operating Rod

The operating rod had to open the bolt by itself after the operating rod spring and guide were removed and the muzzle elevated 60 degrees. It also had to close the bolt when the barrel was lowered 60 degrees past horizontal (Figure 3-13).

Rear Sight

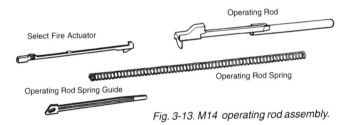

Fig. 3-13. M14 operating rod assembly.

The M14 National Match rear sight was similar to the National Match rear sight developed for the M1 Garand (Figure 3-14). The M14 rear sight was scribed in meters whereas the M1 Garand sight was calibrated in yards. The M14 National Match base can be distinguished by its marking, "NM/2A." The elevation and windage knobs had to move independently of one another and had to produce definite audible clicks. The elevation and windage knobs also had to hold their set positively. The elevation knob had to be at the 100 meter setting when raised 8 clicks from the lowest setting.

A plastic cap was provided to protect the aperture assembly.

Windage: A major functional difference between the M14 standard and the M14 National Match sights lies in the fact that the windage knob threads were changed from 32 to 64 threads per inch (5/16-64 NS-3) for the National Match sight which allowed a 1/2 minute of angle change in windage.

Elevation: Each click of the National Match elevation knob provided a 1/2 minute of angle change in the sight line (0.291

centimeters at 100 meters or 0.5238 inches at 100 yards). The National Match aperture was hooded to prevent glare and reflection in shooter's eye. The hood turned 180 degrees to produce 1/2 minute angle of changes in elevation. This was accomplished by forming the aperture so that it was 0.002 inches longer vertically. When rotated clockwise, the sight line was raised 1/2 minute of angle; when rotated counterclockwise, the sight line was lowered 1/2 minute of angle. The eyepiece held its position by virtue of two spring-loaded balls that engaged a vertical "V" notch in the face of the aperture. The position of the eyepiece was marked by a notch in the rear face.

Aperture: Two aperture diameters were available, #7791133 (1005-864-2926) had a diameter of 0.0595 inches and #7791282 (1005-8642928) had a diameter of 0.0520 inches (Figure 3-15). The eyepiece selected was fitted to the aperture and the AMC recommended that no attempt be made to dismount it and refit the other eyepiece. Instead, the aperture assembly was to be changed.

Changing apertures required the disassembly of the rear sight mechanism. Extreme care had to be taken when handling the parts. The fine pitch threads (64 per inch) on both the windage knob and rear sight base were easily damaged.

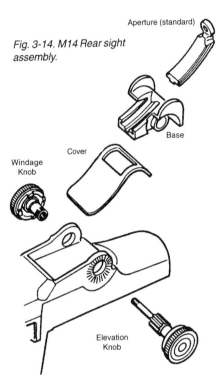

Fig. 3-14. M14 Rear sight assembly.

Changing the National Match Sight Aperture:

1. Insert rear sight base through the opening of the cover.
2. Place the cover's front lip into the recess at the forward portion of rear sight receiver well. Raise the base slightly, exposing the rear portion of the cover. With a screwdriver, apply pressure to rear of the cover in a horizontal direction until it snaps into place and is firmly retained by the receiver.
3. Insert the aperture into the aperture groove in the base and lower until it bottoms against the receiver.
4. Exercise care when starting windage knob threads into the rear sight base to preclude danger of cross threading. Mating threads must be free of excess oil and all foreign matter.

5. With the left hand, apply pressure to the base forward and to the right of the receiver. Insert and turn the windage knob carefully to engage to the mating threads. Continue to turn the knob until the base is tightly seated against the right receiver ear.

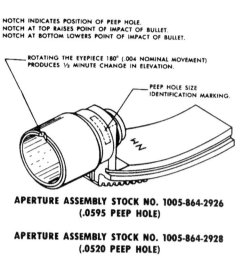

APERTURE ASSEMBLY STOCK NO. 1005-864-2926
(.0595 PEEP HOLE)

APERTURE ASSEMBLY STOCK NO. 1005-864-2928
(.0520 PEEP HOLE)

Fig. 3-15. M14 National match sight aperature assembly.

6. Insert the elevating knob assembly pinion through the hole on left side of receiver ear, meshing the pinion teeth with mating teeth of the aperture.
7. Look inside the axis of the windage knob and find the "flat." Rotate the elevation pinion knob to the corresponding position and thread the rear sight nut (in the windage knob) onto the pinion shaft. (Some manipulation of parts may be necessary). Tighten the rear sight nut until both elevating and windage knobs become inoperative.
8. Back off the rear sight nut one or more clicks. Both knobs will then operate. The graduation mark can now be aligned with the index mark on the receiver.
9. Tighten the rear sight screw securely. Settings of various ranges are attained in terms of the number of clicks from the lowest position of the aperture once the sight has been "zeroed" in at the respective ranges. Once sight settings have been established, the rear sight mechanism should be left intact to preserve the sight's zero.

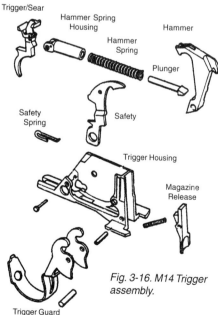

Fig. 3-16. M14 Trigger assembly.

Trigger Assembly

The trigger assembly (Figure 3-16) was especially tuned and honed for the National Match Rifle. The trigger pull was set between 4.5 and 6 lbs and no creep was allowed. The hammer, trigger and sear contact were usually polished to remove the phosphate (parkerized) coating. The safety had to move freely without binding on the hammer. It had to provide a positive lock on the hammer when engaged.

When the trigger assembly was clamped into place, definite resistance had to be encountered 3/8 inches from the locked position.

Table 5
Testing the National Match Rifle

Function Firing: Prior to targeting and accuracy tests, ten rounds were fired from the rifle for functioning. If any malfunction occurred, the rifle was rejected. During the following accuracy and targeting tests, a total of 62 additional rounds were fired. If the rifle malfunctioned, it was rejected.

Accuracy Firing: A pneumatic mount was used at Rock Island Arsenal as the standard machine rest to target and accuracy check all production National Match rifles. In this firing fixture, the weapon was positioned on a cushion locator at the rear bottom of the stock and on a V-Block near front end of the stock behind the rear of the sling swivel. Two steel jaws, lined with rubber cushions were pneumatically operated to rigidly clamp and hold the weapon in position for firing. The weapon recoiled in the firing fixture, under spring tension, and returned to its original position ready to fire the next round.

With the rifle supported in a machine rest, five ten-shot groups were fired at 100 yards for accuracy using match quality ammunition. The average extreme spread of these groups could not exceed 3.5 inches. Any one ten-shot group making this average could not exceed 5.0 inches extreme spread. If these requirements were not met the rifle was rejected.

Targeting Tests: The targeting test insured that the center of impact of a group fired from the rifle was centered on the target with adequate adjustments remaining in elevation and windage. At a range of 100 yards with the rear sight at 8 clicks up from its lowest position, the windage scale at zero, the sights aligned at 6 o'clock on a 5.0 inch bulls eye two shots were fired. If these shots fell right or left of the center of the bull in excess of 5.8 inches, the front sight was adjusted to bring the shots within limitations.

Targeting information was obtained simultaneously with accuracy firing. These accuracy test groups had to fall within a rectangle 11.6 inches horizontal by 17.6 inches vertical, concentrically centered on the bulls eye.

4: THE M21 SNIPER RIFLE

In spite of the popular characterization of the U.S. military as a force of sharp-shooting riflemen dating from 1776, the opposite is in fact true. Until 1855, the U.S. Army maintained only one or at the most, two regiments of soldiers equipped with rifles. The majority of soldiers were issued smoothbore muskets and taught to fire by platoon or company. And until The War in Vietnam, little real effort was placed behind the development of an effective sniper rifle, and just as importantly, the development of a training program for snipers that emphasized field craft as well as accuracy.

Early American Sniper Rifles

The first serious attempt by the Army to develop a sniper rifle began with the Model 1903 Springfield rifle shortly before World War I. A Warner-Swazey telescopic sight was mounted on a bracket bolted to the left side of the receiver on first the Model 1903 Springfield (Figure 4-1) and later, during the war, on the Model 1917 Enfield.

Fig. 4-1. The US Army's first official sniper rifle was the Model 1903 Springfield mounting the Warner-Swazey telescopic sight. (North Cape Collection).

The box-like Warner-Swazey sight (Figure 4-2) proved too delicate and cumbersome for combat and after the war, the Army and the Marine Corps experimented with tubular telescopic sights manufactured by Lyman. The testing was conducted at such a low level that on the eve of American entry into World War II in December 1941, the Army still did not possess an effective sniper rifle.

Fig. 4-2. The Warner-Swazey sight was too delicate for the rough use it saw in the field. (North Cape Collection)

The U.S. Army had adopted the M1 Garand semi-automatic rifle in 1936 and during World War II, it was issued along with the Model 1903A3 Springfield as manufactured by Remington and Smith Corona, and the M1 Carbine. The Army developed sniper versions of all three weapons. The first to be issued was the Model 1903A4 built by Remington (Figure 4-3). Barrels were selected for adherence to close tolerances. A telescopic sight supplied by the Weaver Company and based

Fig. 4-3. The Model 1903 Springfield as built by Remington during World War II was the basis of the Model 1903A4 Sniper rifle. (North Cape Collection)

on their Model 330C, was designated M73B1 by the Ordnance Department. Mounts and rings were supplied by the Redfield Corporation. The 2.2 power scope was barely sufficient for its intended use but the M1903A4 was widely issued from 1942 (Figure 4-4).

Fig. 4-4. The Weaver 330C telescopic sight was militarized as the B73B1 for use with the M1904A4 Sniper Rifle. (North Cape Collection)

The U.S. Marine Corps had developed a sniper version of the earlier M1903A1 Springfield by selecting rifles of proven accuracy that had been built for National Match competition. A long, eight-power telescopic sight manufactured by the Unertl Company (Figure 4-5) was mounted. Less than 1,000 were hand-built at the Marine Base at Quantico, and all that survived have become much sought-after collector's pieces. During much of World War II, Marine snipers also used the Remington M1903A4 sniper rifle.

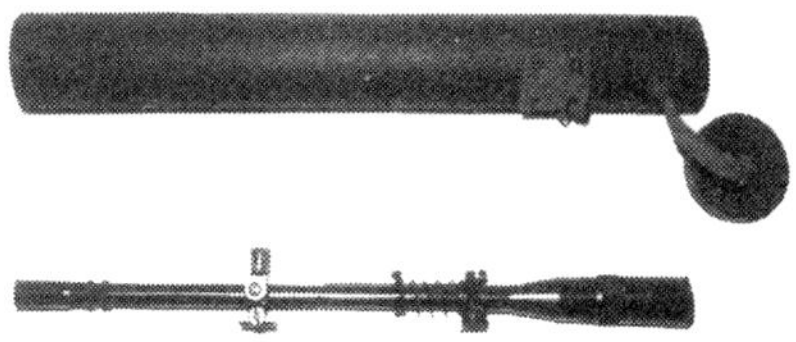

Several attempts were made to develop a sniper version of the M1 Carbine, designated the M1E7. But difficulties in mounting the sight so that it did not interfere with ejec-

Fig. 4-5. The Unertl 8x telescopic sight was selected by the US Marine Corps for use on their Model 1903A1 Sniper Rifles. (North Cape Collection)

tion, and the carbine's short range made the effort hardly worth while and further development was dropped. Another variation, designated the T3, and later the M3, utilized the M1 Carbine with an infrared sniper scope. The M3 was not standardized until August 16, 1945. It saw little or no use in World War II but with an improved infrared illuminating source, was used during the Korean War.

M1C, M1D and MC52 Sniper Rifles.

In response to pressure from the combat forces, the U.S. Army finally decided in mid-1944 to develop a sniper version of the M1 Garand. At Springfield Armory, John C. Garand, the designer of the M1 Garand, began work on a sniper version of his famous rifle. Because the M1 loaded cartridges and ejected spent cases through the top of the receiver, a telescopic sight could not be mounted vertically in line with the bore. Garand, working with engineers at Griffin & Howe, developed an offset bracket and mount system that bolted to the side of the receiver. A larger telescopic sight than the Weaver M73B1 was supplied by the Lyman Corporation, a militarized version of their commercial "Alaskan" hunting sight, given the military designation, M81. The scope was offset to the left of the receiver which still allowed the rifle to be loaded and eject spent cases in the conventional way. The new sniper rifle, designated the M1C was not ready for issue until the late spring of 1945, and consequently, it saw little combat use during World War II (Figure 4-6)

Shortly after he began work on the M1C, John Garand designed a less complicated mount. Instead of attaching to the side of the receiver as with the Griffen and Howe bracket and mount, it encircled the barrel just ahead of the receiver and had a flat side with a threaded hole and two locating pin holes. The telescopic sight was clamped into a bracket that screwed into the mount. The new mount was sturdier and allowed the telescopic sight to be removed without affecting its "zero." The M1 Garand with the new mounting

Fig. 4-6. The M1C was the sniper version of the M1 Garand, the US military's first semiautomatic battle rifle. (North Cape Collection)

system was designated the M1D. Although it was developed by mid-1945, it saw no service in World War II.

The original M81 telescopic sight employed a thin cross hair reticle that snipers complained was often hard to distinguish against a dark background or in low light level conditions. Lyman supplied a new scope, the M82, which had a single post protruding from the bottom.

During the Korean War, many M1C sniper rifles were

recalled and refurbished at the National Armory at Springfield, then shipped to the fighting forces in Korea. Many had new barrels installed as part of the refurbishment process. The M1C, the M1903A4 and the Marine Corps M1903A1 with the 8X Unertl Scope were all issued and saw extensive service during the Korean War.

None of the three World War II-vintage sniper rifles proved effective enough to satisfy either service. The telescopic sights were too delicate and cumbersome and the service rifles used were really not capable of the accuracy de-

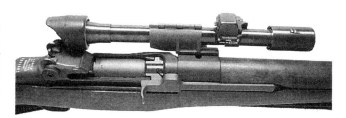

Fig. 4-7. The M1D was an improvement on the M1C in that it used a better reticle pattern and a less-labor intensive telescopic mounting. (Woody Travis collection)

manded for shots in the 400 to 600 yard range. In 1951, an attempt was made to improve the M1C by adding a newly-improved telescopic sight designated the M84. It had a cross hair reticle combined with the solid post. The windage and elevation controls were made larger and easier to adjust and were protected by sturdy snap-over covers. The M84 was also mounted on the M1D (Figure 4-7).

The Marine Corps adopted the M1C Garand as a sniper rifle during the Korean War but they replaced the issue scope with a new 4X scope developed by the Stith Kollmorgen Company as the 4XD MC-1 Telescopic Sight. The new sniper rifle was designated the Marine Corps Model 1952, or MC1952 for short.

But three basic problems with the M1 Garand as a sniper rifle remained: 1) The telescopic sight had to be offset to the left, 2) the telescopic sights developed were only marginally effective and 3) the M1 Garand lacked sufficient range as a true sniper rifle. In fact, an additional problem of similar magnitude lay in the fact that neither the Army nor the Marine Corps had an effective program for training snipers in either the special and demanding types of marksmanship required, or in field craft—the ability to move silently and unobserved close to, or behind enemy lines.

Between the Korean War and the early years of the War in Vietnam, work on an effective sniper rifle languished. The M1D Garand remained the "sniper rifle" with only minimal changes being made to it as a result of the National Match program. The only improvement made after 1954 was the adoption of the a new flash-hider, the T37, which replaced the ungainly M2 cup-shaped flash-hider. The T37 was held onto the barrel by the gas valve screw while the M2, a modified grenade launcher, was held on the muzzle by clamping it to the bayonet mount.

Before and during the early years of the War in Vietnam, informal sniping programs developed in both the Army and Marine Corps. The Army issued M1Ds, ostensibly for use by Republic of Vietnam Army troops. The Marines procured Winchester Model 70s and Remington Model 700s during the 1950s and early 1960s and equipped them with a variety of telescopic sights for match target shooting. But a good many of these rifles and scopes found their way into American Army and Special forces units (Figure 4-8).

Fig. 4-8. Both the Army and the Marine Corps acquired a number of Remington and Winchester bolt action rifles during the 1950s and 1960s for marksmanship training. USMC photo

ally assembled by individuals, 2) National Match M14 rifles equipped with the World War II/Korean War era M84 telescopic sight in mounts developed by the Limited Warfare Laboratory at Aberdeen Proving Grounds, Maryland and the Army Marksmanship Training Unit (AMTU) and 3) M14 match grade rifles equipped with the 3x-9x Adjustable Ranging Telescopic sight (ART) as manufactured by Redfield and designated the "XM21, Sniper with Adjustable Ranging Telescope and Mount."

The massive buildup of U.S. troops in Vietnam occasioned some confusion over equipment and weapons selection. Sniper rifles were not perceived as a high priority weapon system in the early days when establishing a troop presence and securing areas from Vietcong and North Vietnamese Army control was paramount.

To Colonel Frank Conway, USA, assigned as Ordnance Officer to the AMTU at Fort Benning, Georgia, belongs the lion's share of credit for organizing and forcing the development of the M14 sniper rifle system. Overcoming a lack of organizational jurisdiction, apathy and confusion, he established the AMTU as the most knowledgeable agency in the Army as far as sniper rifles and tactics were concerned. Col. Conway forced the adoption of the AMTU's National Match specifications (slightly revised) as the standard for the M14 sniper rifle.

The authority for producing the AMTU version of the M14 for sniper use was entitled "DA MSG 897570, 14 February 1969, For Sniper Rifles and Scopes for use in The Republic of Vietnam," codenamed ENSURE 240 (Expediting Non-Standard Urgent Requirement for Equipment No. 240). Also attached was authorization to develop the adjustable ranging telescope and its mount in cooperation with the Limited Warfare Laboratory and Redfield. The AMTU accuracy specifications for the M14 National Match Rifle are described in Appendix D.

After extensive field testing of the XM21 Sniper Rifle System in Vietnam by the 9th Infantry Division during which final specifications were worked out and training parameters established, the Army adopted the M14 as the M21 Sniper rifle (Figure 4-9).

As the Vietnam War dragged on, the demand for an accurate sniper rifle rose to a crescendo. The Army accordingly instituted an evaluation and selection program that also tested the M1903A4 Springfield equipped with an M84 scope, the M1D and even the M16A1 equipped with a 3X Colt scope designed by the Realist Corporation. The program resulted in the adoption of specially reconfigured M14 rifles. The M14 was selected partly for its ability to provide a quick second shot and partly for its range. The Army Marksmanship Training Unit (AMTU) was charged with turning the M14 into an effective sniper rifle, which they did by applying the accurizing principals worked out for the National Match M14 rifles.

Project ENSURE 240

The road to the standardization of the M14 as the M21 Sniper Rifle System was long and torturous. By 1973, when the last combat troops left Vietnam, three major variations of the M14 sniper rifle had been fielded: 1) standard infantry M14 rifles equipped with a variety of commercial telescopic sights, usu-

The ART Telescopic Sight

A new and modern telescopic sight was developed by Captain James Leatherwood and perfected by Franklin Owens of, and manufactured by, the Limited Warfare Laboratory (LWL) at Aberdeen Proving Ground, Maryland. He termed it the Adjustable Ranging Telescopic (ART) sight. The ART scope had an exterior cam which allowed the shooter to dial in the correct angle of elevation for the M118 7.62 x 51 mm ammunition used by snipers, for any range between 300 and 900 meters.

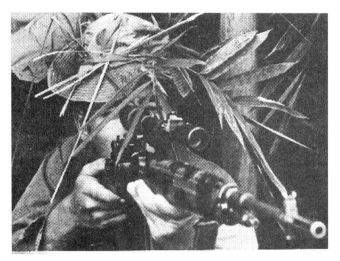

Fig. 4-9. An Army sniper in training in Vietnam. US Army photo

According to Peter Senich in his excellent study of sniping in Vietnam ("The Long Range War: Sniping in Vietnam"), three variations of the Leatherwood scope were used. The first was a Redfield variable power 3x-9x telescopic sight with Accu-Range modified by altering the reticle and attaching a ballistic cam and locking device to a "tool room" version two-piece base manufactured at LWL for testing. The second was a "transitional" model which employed a second generation Redfield 3x-9x redesigned by the LWL in early to mid-1968. In this version, the ballistic cam, power-adjusting ring and lock functioned as a single unit. A one-piece mount was also used. Mounted on accurized M14 rifles, they were sent to Vietnam for field testing by the 9th Infantry Division in September 1968.

The third variation used an adjustable ranging telescope based on the Leatherwood principle which was wholly manufactured by Redfield with the mount fabricated at Frankford Arsenal, Pennsylvania. Mr. Senich points out that except for the identification plate which read (3X-9X AR TEL SEA NO XXX), its black matte rather than shiny black commercial finish and a new mounting plate with rounded corners, it was essentially identical to the second variation. The last three or four digits of the rifle's serial number were engraved on the telescope's side plate and the side or top of the mount.

The practice of engraving the rifle's serial number on mount and scope led to some problems later in Vietnam. Because there were no spare parts available, when a problem occurred with the scope or mount, the entire weapon system was declared unserviceable because unit armorers were reluctant to separate them. This led to an artificially high attrition rate and caused authorities up the chain of command to question the usefulness of the M21 concept. In June of 1970, the AMTU assumed responsibility for the maintenance of the M21 system and immediately informed everyone connected that the serial numbering had only been done for production reasons and there was, therefore, no reason not to separate the components. This allowed unit armorers to mount serviceable scopes on other M21 rifles and so keep as many units operational in the field as possible.

As a point of information, James Leatherwood, the inventor of the adjustable ranging principal, was not involved with the manufacture of the ART scopes used during the Vietnam War. After retiring as a captain from the U.S. Army, he was employed by Realist and later Military Armament Corporation before founding Leatherwood Brothers to further develop, produce and market a rifle scope for combat use. A second generation, ART II scope was developed by 1978 and in 1980, the first direct sale of his scopes was made to the U.S. Army. The following year, Leatherwood Brothers developed a new variation known as the ART/MPC which required only a single cam for a "wide variety of rifle cartridges."

The M21 Replaced

In spite of the fact that the War in Vietnam was raging during its development, the M21 Sniper Rifle was primarily designed to be used in the somewhat restricted killing grounds of Europe. The M1C/D Garand had been considered a 400 yard sniper rifle and the M21 a 600 yard sniper rifle. As the Cold War was ending in the late 1980s, a new military threat to the United States and its allies and friends developed in the Middle East. A thousand yard sniper rifle was required and as later experience proved in the Persian Gulf War (1990-91), snipers had an important role to play in the wide expanses of desert.

By the mid-1980s, the M21 Sniper Rifles were beginning to wear out and spare parts had become scarce. To extend the life of the M21, the U.S. Army's 10th Special Forces group was assigned to develop an "improved" M21. Brookfield Precision Tool designed a stock liner which could be bedded into a McMillan fiberglass stock with steel bedding compound. The barreled action could be removed for cleaning and maintenance more frequently without wearing the bedding. When reseated, the barreled action returned to zero. A Barnett barrel and a Harris bipod attached to the stock were also incorporated. Brookfield Precision Tool also developed a telescopic sight mount that attached to the side of the receiver with an offset screw/lever combination. The mount also slipped into the dovetail slot which normally held the cartridge clip guide.

The M25, as it was designated, was used by all branches of the U.S. military as well as the FBI, DEA and other paramilitary organizations. The M25 has been used in combat from Panama to the Persian Gulf to the Balkans.

But even with the M25 in inventory, it was clear that something more was needed. The Army specifications called for less than minute of angle accuracy to 1,000 meters.

Taking a page from the Marine Corps' book, the Army worked closely with Remington Arms to develop a new "bolt action" sniper rifle that would be designated the M24 Sniper Weapon System (SWS) see Figure 4-10.

The new sniper rifle was based on the Remington Model

Fig. 4-10. A U.S. military sniper on field exercises poses with his M24 SWS rifle.

700 BDL receiver. It mounted a 24-inch stainless steel barrel with a bore specially cut for the M118 7.62 match grade cartridge and bullet. The barrel's 5R rifling was developed by Remington based on the pattern used in the Soviet Army's SVD Dragunov Sniper Rifle (Figure 4-11). It had five lands and grooves making one turn in 11.25 inches (1:11.25) and the edges of the lands were slightly rounded to reduce friction. The stock was a composite of kevlar and graphite with a beaver-tail forearm and a high comb for use with the telescopic sights. The buttplate is adjustable through a range of 2.7 inches to accommodate all shooters. The composite stock does not absorb moisture and provides greater consistency no matter the climatic or weather conditions.

The heavy barrel is free floated — it does not touch any part of the forend. The action is rounded on the bottom and rests in a V-shaped aluminum channel bedded into the stock.

The aluminum channel extends the full-length of the forearm and the sling swivels, magazine floor plate and the trigger guard attach to it for additional strength.

The floor plate can be opened by a release switch inside the trigger guard to quickly dump the ammunition in the five-shot magazine. Like all other metal parts, the floor plate has been given a matte black finish to prevent light reflections.

The Leupold M3 Ultra telescopic sight is a fixed, 10 power scope. It has a range-finding reticle and a built-in compensator for bullet drop. Windage is adjustable in one-half minute of angle increments. The range-finding reticle subtends 0.75 mils. The accessory pack that accompanies the rifle also includes receiver and muzzle bases for back up iron sights, Harris Bipod, Bausch & Lomb Spotting Scope, Laser Range Finder, and Steiner Binoculars and tripod.

Fig. 4-11. SVD Dragunov, the former Soviet Union's chief sniper weapon. In testing by the author, it did not quite show "minute of angle" accuracy. From the collection of John Capalbo.

5: THE CIVILIAN M14S

In 1968, the U.S. Congress passed the comprehensive Gun Control Act. Among its provisions was one specifying that any firearm receiver manufactured for full automatic fire would be considered a machine gun and restricted as such. The law did not allow such receivers to be sold to civilians without special "Title 3" licenses and the payment of a $200 transfer tax. This effectively limited the distribution of M14s by the Director of Civilian Marksmanship via affiliated clubs to a very few civilian high power shooters.

At the same time, the sudden cancellation of the M14 contract left the three private contractors, Winchester, Harrington & Richardson and TRW, plus Springfield National Armory, with large inventories of now useless parts. To recoup some of their investment, they sold parts in excess of military spares requirements for scrap on the open market.

Meanwhile, civilian high power shooters had been suffering in the National Matches. They were allowed to shoot the M14 in the matches but they could not —

Fig. 5-1. Springfield, Inc.'s M1A rifle. Photo courtesy of Springfield, Inc.

except in rare cases — possess an M14 for training and practice. This meant that their only familiarization came during a few hours practice crammed in before a match and this placed them at a distinct disadvantage to military personnel who were able to practice with the M14 rifle at any time.

Springfield Inc.

Elmer Ballance of the L.H. Gun Company in Devine, Texas, saw a potential market. He managed to acquire a large stock of surplus M14 parts and contracted with Valley Ordnance, Wilkes-Barre, Pennsylvania to manufacture new, investment-cast receivers without the sear shaft and sear release housing—which provided the mount for the selector switch. The

Bureau of Alcohol, Tobacco and Firearms approved the receiver and the new rifles went on sale as the M1A in September 1971. The following month, AR Sales of South El Monte, California produced their version, designated the Mark IV. Like the L.H. Gun Company rifle, its receiver was investment cast from 8620 steel alloy.

The Springfield National Armory ceased operations on April 30, 1968. In an effort to gain additional acceptance, the L.H. Gun Company adopted the name, "Springfield Armory." An estimated 2,000 rifles of what have become known as the "Devine Springfield" were subsequently sold under the name, Springfield Armory®. They can be identified by the marking on the underside of the barrel, "RT 1, BX 210, DEVINE TX".

Sales were slower than anticipated but some effective lobbying with the National Rifle Association achieved a rule change for high power matches allowing commercially-manufactured versions of the M14 rifle to be used (Figure 5-1). But the rule change did not take effect soon enough to help the L.H. Gun Company. To cut costs, in June 1974, the company moved production facilities to San Antonio, Texas. The rifles manufactured there were marked with the barrel address "12106 RADIUM WAY SA TEX 78216" By October 1974, the company was near the end of its resources and it was sold.

Production facilities were moved once again, this time to Geneseo, Illinois. Match grade barrels were produced by Numrich Arms of West Hurley, New York and were marked, "GENESEO, ILL" on the bottom, while the rest of the rifle was assembled from surplus M14 parts. But as the supply of barrels and stocks was exhausted, Springfield was forced to begin producing these parts themselves, either directly or through subcontractors. In the mid-1980s, in an effort to increase their market and offset the poor reputation their rifles had earned because of on-again, off-again quality control problems earlier, Springfield Armory introduced a comprehensive quality assurance program. Almost overnight, the rifles improved. Gunsmiths were sent to rifle matches around the country where they made themselves available to repair the company's products on the spot. The company prospered and expanded its line to include the SAR-48 and SAR-4800, Brazilian-made FALs *(Fusil Leger Automatique)*, the SAR-8, a copy of the Heckler and Koch Model 91 and a line of handguns based on the Government Model 1911A1.

But in 1994, Springfield Armory, Inc., was forced to declare bankruptcy. A reorganization a few months later as Springfield, Inc. allowed them to retain the rights to the registered "Springfield Armory" name and they were soon manufacturing the Springfield M1A again.

Today, Springfield, Inc., is a thriving company and a respected name in the firearms industry, particularly among high power match shooters. Their line of M1A rifles now includes the standard M1A, a shortened "Bush" rifle, "Scout" rifle, National Match, Super Match and Tactical rifles, all with numerous barrel, sight and stock variations. In addition, Springfield, Inc., is a major supplier of shooting accessories, including one of the best telescopic sights available for long range shooting. Through a subsidiary, Rock Island Armory, they are also an excellent source for M14-type receivers, M14 parts kits to be used in building match rifles on commercial receivers, and M14 parts.

Smith Enterprises

Smith Enterprises is well known for their finely machined, if somewhat expensive receivers (Figure 5-2). But they are expensive for a reason. Each receiver is built according to strict standards based on those established by the U.S. Ordnance Department for the M14. Some of the finest match-grade M14-type rifles have been built on Smith receivers. Western Ordnance, the parent company of Smith Enterprises, was founded by Richard Smith, a qualified Master Armorer and metallurgist, in the early 1980s and he worked out the techniques for forging receivers in the same manner as the original Springfield National Armory M14 receivers. Smith Enterprise receivers today are precision investment cast of 8620 steel and double heat treated. The first heat treatment hardens the receiver overall to between 52 and 56 on the Rockwell C scale while the second heat treatment hardens the receiver's surface to 60 Rockwell C, to a depth of 0.002 inches.

Smith Enterprises also produces single and double lugged receivers. The lugs are made of solid bar steel and are welded onto the receiver. They undergo the heat treatment process along with the receiver.

The original Smith Enterprise forged receivers have attained collector's status and today draw a high premium. Richard Smith has recently retired but his son, Ron, maintains that today's precision investment cast receivers are just as care-

fully manufactured and just as rugged and long wearing as the forged receivers. They are manufactured from U.S. Government drawing sheets and meet all applicable military specifications.

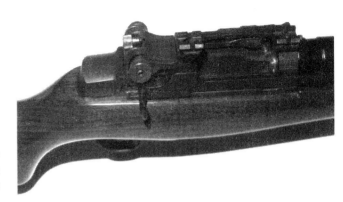

Fig. 5-2. The original Smith Entreprise receiver was drop-forged in the same manner as the original M14 military receivers. Photo courtesy of Smith Enterprise.

In addition to receivers, Smith Enterprises custom builds M14-type match rifles as well as flashhiders, M14-type scope mounts, extended bolt stop releases, National Match sling loops and a number of other products. Further information about Smith Enterprise receivers and other services can be obtain from the company (See Appendix E) or from their Internet web site at www.smithenterprise.com.

Armscorp USA

The Armscorp company began business as the U.S. representative of the South African munitions firm, Armscorp. In the 1980s, when all South African products were embargoed as a result of that nation's continuing policy of apartheid, Armscorp cut all ties with the South African firm and reformed as an American manufacturer of M14 receivers. Over the past sixteen years, the company, under the leadership of Jack Friese, has become a major manufacturer of semiautomatic M14-type receivers and custom-built match rifles.

Investment cast of 8620 alloy, the same type of steel as the original M14 receivers, the Armscorp receiver is offered in the standard configuration as well as with single and double-lugs. Armscorp holds all military specifications in their manufacture but with certain enhancements. For instance, the rail for the bolt roller is cut differently so that the bolt roller does not slam back as in the original M14 receiver. Also, the rail is 1/16th inch wider. Armscorp USA was also the first to offer single and double lugged receivers which can be bedded more solidly to improve accuracy. In addition to receivers, Armscorp also offers finished rifles in both standard and match grade — although the emphasis lately has been on match grade rifles. Each rifle is built one at a time by Armscorp's custom gunsmiths and the quality is more than evident.

Several Armscorp receivers were examined and discussions were conducted with several gunsmiths. We found them to be of uniformly high quality and well-finished. Not one gunsmith we talked with found a major fault in the receivers whether it was regarding, fit, finish or materials. In fact, several were enthusiastic in their praise and more than one exhibited a very fine match grade rifle built on an Armscorp receiver.

Fig. 5-3. This fine Match Grade M14-Type rifle was built by custom gunsmith Evan Carolyn and produced a 100 yard, three shot group that measured .045 inches. (From the collection of Phil Cuevas)

Our own experience bore this out. We procured two rifles built on Armscorp receivers. The first was built by Evelyn Carolyn, a custom gunsmith in Orange, California. Using a double-lugged receiver, a Krieger barrel, a Leupold Ultra M3 10x telescopic sight, National Match Sights and a stock of his own manufacture, he produced one of the finest match M14-type rifles we have seen to date (Figure 5-3). Firing Federal Gold Medal match ammunition, we produced a five shot, 100 yard group measuring just 0.45 inches center to center and at 300 yards, 1.95 inches center to center.

The second rifle was built by Armscorp as their

Fig. 5-4. Armscorp's M21 Match Rifle built with a rear-lugged receiver is guaranteed to shoot less than 1 MOA at 100 yards. It did in our tests.

M21 Match Rifle. It used a rear-lugged receiver solidly bedded in a McMillan black fiberglass stock and was equipped with national match sights (Figure 5-4). Armscorp guarantees that their M21 rifle will shoot less than 1 MOA at 100 yards. Rarely have we shot an M14-type rifle that settled into position so comfortably and shot so accurately, right out of the box. After a fifty round break-in period with frequent cleaning, the bore was decoppered and using Federal Gold Medal Match (168 grain spire point bolt tail bullets) and iron sights, at 100 yards from a rest, five shot groups averaging 1.15 inches were shot, the best our aging eyes could do. After an ART II scope was mounted on Armscorp's steel scope mount and sighted in, three five shot groups averaged 0.69 inches at 100 yards and

2.55 inches at 300 yards. We were quite certain that as the rifle settles in, that the group sizes would continue to close down. Armscorp was certainly in no danger of having to make good on their guarantee with this rifle.

The Entréprise Arms M14A2 Receiver

Entréprise Arms of Irwindale, California is currently manufacturing an M14-style receiver machined from a solid billet of 8620 steel. The receivers are made to original Springfield National Armory specifications and are based on original M14 drawings.

Solid blocks of 8620 steel weighing 12.5 pounds are secured in a CNC milling machine jig. Five separate operations are automatically performed on the steel block that roughs the receiver to shape. The rough receiver is then transferred to the next CNC-milling machine which performs six more milling operations. The final five milling and drilling operations are performed in a third CNC-controlled machine which produces a ready-for-final-polishing, hardening and finishing, receiver (Figure 5-5). The process takes minutes rather than hours and the end result is a finished receiver that matches the original M14 specifications established by the U.S. Army Ordnance Department at Springfield National Armory in 1957, in every respect.

After the machining operations, the receiver is sent to quality control for gauging and measuring. Entréprise uses the same Quality Control specifications that were applied to the M14 receivers made at the National Armory at Springfield, Massachusetts, at Harrington and Richardson, Winchester and TRW when the original M14 was being built in the 1960s.

All Entréprise M14A2 receivers are exterior hardened to 55-57 Rockwell C to a depth of 1/20,000 of an inch, as were the original receivers. The receivers are then polished to remove tool marks. The Entréprise M14A2 receiver is finished in a Mil-Spec parkerizing, but can also be had in a black oxide finish by custom gunsmiths who intend to build custom match rifles and want to refinish the receivers to their own preferences.

Introduced in mid-1996, the Entréprise M14A2 has already gained a following among custom gunsmiths specializing in M14 match rifles. See the Directory in Appendix E for the addresses and phone numbers of the firms mentioned above. Also see their Internet web site at www.entreprise.com.

Fig. 5-5. The progression from solid steel billet (top) to final form (bottom) of the Entréprise receiver is shown in this photograph.

Building M14A2 Rifles

But manufacturing a fine receiver is only one factor in building an M14-type rifle. How well do M14 parts kits (available from various sources) mate to the receiver? Will the fee charged rise astronomically because parts have to be fitted, holes redrilled for pins, screw holes redrilled and tapped, or metal cut away to mate parts into the receiver properly?

Both John Capalbo of Garden Grove, California and James Gronning of Grúning Precision, Riverside, California were asked to assemble M14-type rifles on Entréprise M14A2 receivers at our request. Parts used were from original M14 rifles that had been disassembled. All parts were original and in excellent condition. Both John Capalbo and Jim Gronning are experienced M14 gunsmiths, having built numerous service and match grade M14-type rifles previously for clients. John Capalbo was asked to build a service grade rifle and Jim Gronning, a mid-range and a long range match grade rifle, the former using a Canadian Arsenals (Long Branch) National Match barrel and the latter commercial Kreiger match grade barrel.

Service Grade M14-type Rifle

The most important aspect of building any rifle is mating the barrel and receiver. Any gunsmith will tell you that this is where most problems occur, particularly with semiautomatic rifles. For starters, the barrel threads must match the threads cut in the receiver. Next, the barrel must "index" properly, i.e., it must screw into the receiver exactly the correct distance to allow the front sight to be vertical in relation to the centerline of the receiver and the rear sights. Also, the chamber in the breech end of the barrel must be positioned properly so that the cartridge "head spaces" correctly.

Both gunsmiths reported no problems installing the barrels on the Entréprise M14A2 receivers. Both barrels required only truing before installation. In both instances, the rear sight was assembled onto the receiver and the alignment with the front sight checked using a centering guide. No further barrel work was required. A walnut M14 surplus stock in excellent condition was used on the service grade rifle (Figure 5-6). A fiberglass handguard was added. For the match grade rifle—and in keeping with the receiver's M14A2 designation — a TRW-manufactured fiberglass stock was used.

Fiberglass stocks were scheduled to replace the wooden stocks on the M14 rifles but the rifle was withdrawn from service before the changeover could be completed. The non-porus fiberglass stock eliminates many of the "wandering point of aim" problems encountered with the original M14 wooden stock as it absorbed and lost moisture.

Fig. 5-6. Custom gunsmith John Capalbo mates the trigger assembly to a service grade M14-type rifle built on an Entréprise receiver. (Author's collection)

The trigger assembly slid into place in both rifles without problems and latched down with some effort, assuring a tight fit in the stock. Headspace checks on both rifles showed that their chambers were well within the limits specified by the U.S. Ordnance Department — 1.6355 to 1.6385 inches (See sidebar at end of Chapter). Total time to assemble the completed service rifle was less than twenty-five minutes.

Mid-Range M14-Type Rifle

Jim Gronning spent considerably more time building our match grade rifle. Because we also wanted to test the accuracy of the rifle in a military issue, fiberglass stock, we did not glass bed this rifle. Instead, we selected our fiberglass stock by inserting the match-grade barreled receiver into some twenty-two stocks (surplus military stocks, some of which had seen a great deal of use) before we found one that fit tightly and without slip in any direction.

Jim then unitized the gas cylinder assembly, reworked the trigger group to National Match standards and installed National Match front and rear sights (Figure 5-7).

Nationally respected custom gunsmith, Clint Fowler, known for his excellent match M14 and M1 Garand rifles, uses both Springfield and Armscorp receivers in building his successful match M14-type rifles. In the M14, he prefers to work with double lugged rifles. After testing all four commercial receivers currently available, and listening to a wide variety of custom gunsmiths, it seems to us that choosing a particular receiver for a match grade M14-type rifle should depend on other require-

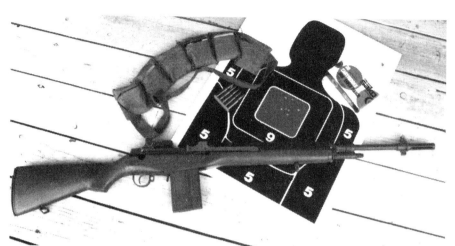

Fig. 5-7. Custom gunsmith Jim Gronning's match grade M14-type mid-range (400-600 yards) rifle in a fiberglass M14A1 stock, built on an Entréprise receiver. The target was fired at 200 yards with iron sights. (Author's collection).

ments than the physical construction, dimensional tolerance and materials of any of the four receivers discussed above. Each will produce a superb rifle in the hands of a custom gunsmith experienced in building M14-type match rifles.

1000 Yard Match Rifle

Following our success with a semi-custom match rifle, a custom long range match rifle was built from scratch to include the following:

* 1/2 minute of angle accuracy with match ammunition.
* meet all requirements for CMP and NRA service rifle matches and M14 National Match characteristics.
* bedded receiver that would last at least 10,000 rounds.
* stainless steel National Match barrel or equivalent.
* National Match rear sights capable of 1/2 minute of angle adjustment.
* fiberglass stock fitted to my reach and configuration.
* provision for the attachment of a telescopic sight for non-match shooting.

Again, my choice of a custom gunsmith was Jim Gronning of Grúning Precision. He had already built a custom Elk rifle for me as well as the mid-range custom M14-type match rifle described in the previous paragraphs. Mindful that a gunsmith's most precious asset is his time, I reviewed the list of the features I wanted on my rifle. Jim listened without comment as I went through them, then offered suggestions regarding the type and manufacturer for specific items. He also suggested a few changes. When we thought we had hashed out everything necessary, Jim prepared a cost estimate and went to work.

He began with an Entréprise M14A2 receiver in the white. His first step was to mill the front face absolutely square. He then added a full lug welded to the rear, and a front lug. One of the secrets of the phenomenal accuracy from Jim's M14-type lugged rifles comes from the fact that he uses a front lug of his own design that is attached without welding. He does not like to apply welding temperature heat at the receiver's face around the sensitive barrel thread and lug area, see Figure 5-8. The lugs were drilled and tapped for screws which would secure the receiver to the stock. This procedure provides a more precise receiver/stock alignment and vastly increases bedding life.

A Krieger match barrel was selected and cryogenically stress-relieved. The barrel had already been turned to final shape but it needed a chamber. Jim does not like to use short-chambered barrels but prefers to cut his own chambers to his own formula, another key to the extreme accuracy of his rifles.

Fig. 5-8. The Grúning Precision front lug slides over the barrel and is held hard against the receiver face by a shoulder. This avoids the application of heat to the sensitive receiver face.

The M14-type rifle's front sight is mounted on the flashhider. But under California's new 1999 Assault Rifle law, flashhiders are one count toward making your rifle an assault weapon, requiring registration. We had no choice but to install a standard M14 flashhider, reamed to National Match standards. If and when the California Department of Justice decides to approve a non-flashhider barrel extension, it would be a simple task to replace it. If not, other provisions will have to be made.

The receiver was blued rather than Parkerized. Parkerizing requires that the surface be lightly sand blasted and this creates a certain amount of unnecessary friction in rubbing areas. The barrel was installed and the bolt fitted and its lugs lapped.

Jim installed a National Match rear sight with a spring and ball detent to eliminate side-to-side play. The B. Jones lens

place to prevent the bedding from being crushed by over tightening the stock screws and poured the bedding compound into the stock. The barreled receiver was settled into the stock, the barrel located dead center in the forend and the trigger assembly inserted for placement. The front and rear stock screws were inserted and torqued to 40 inch pounds at the front and 50

Fig. 5-9. The author's 1000 yard M14-type rifle, built by Jim Gronning, Grúning Precision, Riverside, CA provides subminute of angle groups at extreme ranges.

holder was installed in the aperture and the correct lens for my vision was inserted. Fully approved for service rifle matches, the corrective lens meant that I no no longer need to wear eye glasses while shooting the rifle. Bob Jones, the owner of the company, provides lenses in any correction and in a wide variety of colors for different shooting conditions.

Jim next reworked a standard M14 trigger assembly to National Match standards. He disassembled the trigger group, cleaned and polished all moving parts and trued angles where necessary. The sear received a careful polishing. When reinstalled, the trigger and sear tripped at exactly 4.85 pounds.

The front barrel band and gas cylinder were unitized using the USMC method of welding. An oversized operating guide rod was installed and the sling swivel was mounted in the forearm using two star nuts. No matter how hard the sling is drawn up, it will not pull loose from the forearm.

A MacMillan stock in northern woodland camouflage was selected. These fiberglass stocks are among the finest obtainable for the M14/M1A. I particularly like the way the wrist is done. I am a six footer with the average reach for my

Fig. 5-10. An oversized operating rod guide was installed.

height but I also have small-to-medium hands. I find that the MacMillan stock fits me perfectly. No stock liner is used with a MacMillan stock; instead, Jim builds vertical pillars that reinforce the bedding which enfolds the receiver on five sides. Chisels and a power grinder cut away portions of the stock's interior to receive the bedding compound.

After constructing dams to prevent the bedding compound (Steel Devcon) from flowing away, he coated the barreled receiver with mold release agents, set the aluminum pillars in

inch pounds at the rear. The assembly was set aside to dry.

The following day, the barreled receiver was removed from the stock with some difficulty because of the close fit between metal and bedding. A few minutes with a grinder and chisel cleaned up burrs and spurs and beveled sharp edges so that the stock could be removed more easily for maintenance. Jim polished the MacMillan stock then lubricated the receiver with solid film lubricant and replaced it in the stock. The stock bolts were again torqued down to 40 and 50 inch pounds respectively, front and rear —the exact

Fig. 5-11. Aluminum pillars were installed for the rear and front lug screws to prevent overtightening.

amount of pressure for the front and rear bolts will be determined in future shooting tests. The handguard had already been modified to make certain that no part of it touched the barrel.

The flash hider was reamed to specification and mounted on the barrel. The bayonet mount was also removed to prevent the rifle from being used in the drive-by bayonetting if it should be stolen by a gang banger.

I have always been taught that breaking in a new rifle properly was almost as important to accuracy as proper rifling, bedding and a good grade of ammunition. Jim concurred heartily and we followed his method. A clean patch was run through the bore and the first round fired. The bore was then cleaned throughly with solvent-soaked patches, dried and fired again. This was repeated for the first ten shots. For the next ten rounds, the barrel was cleaned after every other round, then cleaned at

Fig. 5-12. The rear lug is welded to the receiver.

the end of the sequence with a de-coppering agent. At that point, we shifted to cleaning after every five rounds. The rifle was now sighted in using the procedure described in Table 11, at the end of Chapter 10.

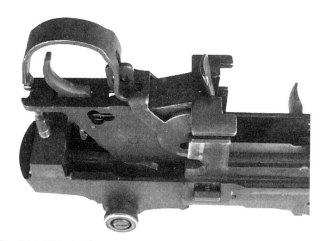

Fig. 5-13. With the front and rear lugs secured to the stock by screws at two points, the trigger assembly no longer acts as a single point clamp. The barreled-action can now be adjusted fore and aft to achieve precise alignment in the stock.

Once the rifle was zeroed, it was cleaned once more and two bore conditioning rounds were fired. Then from a sandbag rest a five shot group was fired at a standard rifle target at 100 yards using M118 match ammunition. We adjusted the torque on the front and rear stock screws, continuing to fire five shot groups until we achieved average five shot groups of 0.45 inches. Outstanding! And we knew the groups would tighten up as the rifle wore in.

The M14-type rifles show their extreme versatility in the three rifles built for this program: standard service rifle which to date has fired more than 3,000 rounds without a fall-off in accuracy; 600 yard match grade rifle *without* a bedded stock and our all out, 1000 yard match rifle complete with bedded

stock. Testing to date with 175 and 178 grain Federal Gold Medal Match ammunition shows consistent sub-minute of angle accuracy at 800 and 1,000 yards.

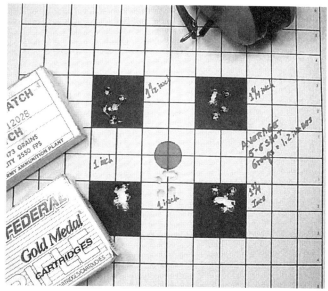

Fig. 5-14. An early test target shot from fixed rest with the long range rifle at 200 yards on a windless day with Federal Match (175 grain): groups sizes varied from 1.0 to 1.5 inches.

How to Check Head Space on the M14 Rifle

Headspace specifications depend on which cartridge is being used.

7.62 x 51 NATO: 1.6355 to 1.6385 inches .

.308 Winchester: 1.630 to 1.638 inches.

If you use commercial head space gages, remove the extractor and ejector from the bolt. (Military headspace gages are relieved for the extractor and ejector and so they do not need to be removed.) Replace the bolt in the receiver but do not replace the operating rod. Insert the "Go" gage into the breech and close the bolt. It should close easily over the "Go" gage. Replace the "Go" gage with the "No Go" gage. Move the bolt forward. The bolt should not close on the "No Go" gage. If the bolt does close on the "No Go" gage, replace it with the "Field Gage." Never fire a rifle if the bolt closes on the "Field Gage."

CAUTION: Do not interchange 7.62 NATO and .308 cartridges. Dimensional differences can create timing difficulties and dangerous breech pressures.

6: CHINESE M14S

Interestingly enough, there are three Chinese-made variations of the M14 rifle. The first was manufactured by the Nationalist Government of Taiwan on machinery and tooling purchased from Harrington & Richardson after the Department of Defense unexpectedly canceled all further acquisition of the M14 in 1964. The second and third variations were manufactured in the People's Republic of China, specifically for sale to American high power rifle shooters in the United States.

Taiwanese M14s

The M14 rifle was adopted by the Republic of China (Taiwan) in 1968. Production actually began in 1969 and continued well into the 1970s to re-equip the Nationalist Army of Taiwan. These rifles are almost identical to the American-made M14, with the exception of their markings, but are wholly made from Taiwanese-manufactured parts fabricated by the State Arsenal of the Republic of China. The rifle was designated the Type 57 in accordance with Nationalist Chinese practice of dating from the year of Dr. Sun Yat-sen's Nationalist Revolution of 1911.

Taiwanese-manufactured M14 rifles are marked in Chinese ideograms in two variations. Type 1 rifles are marked, "Rifle 7.62/Type 57 Made in China," followed by the Arsenal's trademark. Type 2 rifles are marked "Rifle Type 57/Made in Republic of China," also followed by the arsenal trademark (Figure 6-1). Because these rifles were made as selective fire weapons, they are considered "machine guns" by the BATF and their importation and sale to civilian purchasers is not allowed.

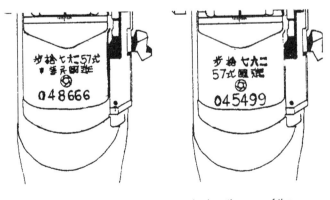

Fig. 6-1. M14s made on Tiawan are marked on the rear of the receiver in Chinese characters, "Rifle Type 57/Made in (Republic of) China." Used with permission, Dr. Edward C. Ezell.

PRC M14s

In the early 1990s, the government of the People's Republic of China (mainland) allowed the manufacture of M14-type rifles for semiautomatic fire only, for export to the United States (Figure 6-2). Two variations of these rifles were offered for sale on the civilian market through two separate combines of companies, one known as Polytech and the other as Norinco. Polytech is subsidiary of the People's Liberation Army. Norinco, which is short for North China Industries, is a collection of 150 separate factories banded together in a marketing arrangement and is a subsidiary of the Ministry of Ordnance Industries.

Fig. 6-2. Chinese-manufactured Polytech M14-type rifle.

A rumor extent for some time and repeated to the author by four different and reliable sources, holds that the Chinese M14s were first manufactured in the 1960s to be supplied to Chinese Special Forces, the Viet Cong and to communist insurgents in the Philippines. At that time, the M14 was the Standard A issue weapon of U.S. forces. It was thought in the PRC that the VC and the Phillipine insurgents would be able to obtain repair parts and additional ammunition from battlefield pickups and by raiding ammunition dumps. The rifles were made without markings except for serial numbers.

The rifles were never delivered and two decades later, after the mounting for the selector assembly was removed, the Chinese government certified them all as having been made for semiautomatic fire only. And exported to the United States.

True or not, both the Norinco and Polytech M14-type rifles are wholly made in mainland China. There have been conflicting reports regarding their suitability for shooting. One report in which the hardness of the Springfield Inc., hammer and bolt were compared to the Polytech hammer and bolt showed quite a difference — the Springfield parts both measured 58 on the Rockwell C scale while the Polytech parts measured 46 and 44 respectively. Springfield receivers measured 50 and the Polytech, 44. Springfield barrels measured 33 while the Polytech barrel was just 29. By way of comparison, the Entréprise M14A2 receiver tested 55 to 57 on the Rockwell C scale.

The softness of the Polytech receiver is borne out by the fact that the military M14, Entréprise and Springfield Inc. receivers both require 200 pounds of torque to seat the barrel properly. This crushes the threads slightly to keep the barrel from turning out. The Polytech barrel on the other hand, is easily seated and is must be held in place with a set screw to keep it from backing out (Figure 6-3). This suggests that receivers are soft enough that lifetimes will be measured in at most, a few thousand rounds.

Fig. 6-3. Polytech M14-type barrels are held in place with a set screw.

Recently, several custom services have offered heat-treating and rehardening services for Polytech receivers. One such company is Smith Enterprises of Tempe, Arizona. The owner, Ron Smith, is a fourth generation armorer and was trained in ordnance manufacturing and metallurgy. He has studied the metallurgical properties of the Chinese receivers and bolts and found them to be made of ordnance grade steel, if somewhat softer than American-made bolts and receivers. Accordingly, he has developed a double heat treating method to harden receivers and bolts, and as this was written, had performed over 2,000 such heat treat operations.

Mr. Smith has found that the Chinese bolts, as received, measure about 40 on the Rockwell C scale while the receivers measure between 45 and 50. After the reheat treatment, bolts and receivers approach the hardness figures of American-made bolts and receivers. In addition to heat treating, Smith Enterprises can remachine the Chinese receivers to accept American-made bolts.

If you intend to purchase a Chinese-made M14-type rifle, you should consider the following. 1) The original composition of the steel used in the Chinese receivers is not widely known and spokespersons for either importer were unable to provide them. 2) The 7.62 mm NATO cartridge develops breech pressures in excess of 50,000 lbs per square inch. 3) You should consider very seriously having the bolt and receiver hardened to American standards by a gunsmith trained in metallurgy and heat treat processes.

Carefully check the headspace before firing it the first time with military standard gauges. Under no circumstances, should the bolt close on the no-go gauge! After fifty rounds, check the headspace again. If you note any lengthening, make certain that it is still within acceptable range and recheck after the next fifty rounds. If you find that the headspace continues to lengthen you will be able to estimate how many rounds remain before the rifle exceeds the maximum head space specification and becomes too dangerous to fire. See page 24 for instructions on checking headspace.

Unfortunately, reports from several custom gunsmiths who have submitted Norinco rifles for metallurgical testing have not been as favorable as those for the Polytech rifles. Receivers are even softer and dimensionally, they are not as well-made as the Polytech M14s. And there have been several reports of head space losses in Norinco M14s after as few as 200 rounds.

Identifying Polytech Parts

Polytech receivers are marked on the rear left side and the area behind the rear sight is left blank. The markings read: M-14S .308/IDE USA SFLD MICH/POLYTECH CHINA Serial #. The only other receiver markings are what appears to be a part number stamped or etched on the right side. The number observed on several receivers was "11554." Flash suppressors are cast, buttplates are cast and show milling marks near the top (Figure 6-4). The castings are fairly rough when compared to U.S. production and the checkered pattern is coarser. Stock wood appears to be beech or catalpa, both serviceable and widely used, but not as dense or hard as walnut

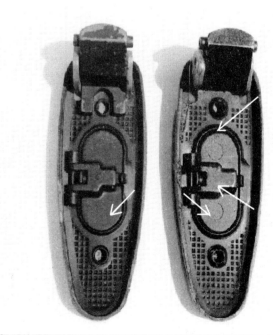

Fig. 6-4. Polytech M14 buttplates (r) show machine marks and the checkering is coarser than American military buttplates (l). Note also the two investment casting dimples on the Polytech buttplate door and the deeper buttplate screwhole flanges.

and completely unmarked by the manufacturer. The softer wood will compress faster than walnut under the jolt of recoil and so for serious shooting, consider a thorough bedding operation (see Chapter 7, Turn Your Commercial M14 into a Match Rifle). Barrels are completely unmarked. Trigger guards appear to have been cast and then machined to final shape. Machining marks are quite evident and again, the only marking was a part number, "044102" etched into the left side (Figure 6-5). No part number or other marking was visible on any of the hammers observed. The bolt was serial numbered to the rifle and the number was etched with an electric pen on the bottom of the bolt. No other marking was observed. Remaining parts were unmarked.

Magazines appeared well made and serviceable and responded well in firing tests. They may or may not fit U.S. made M14-type rifles, depending on the magazine.

Other Considerations

Both the Norinco and Polytech M14 rifles are built using the metric scale of measurement. That means that all screw threads are also metric, as are diameters, widths and lengths. Many Chinese-made parts will fit American-made M14-type rifles but not the other way around.

Chinese parts that are interchangeable with no, or minor, fitting required include the gas cylinder, bolt parts but not the bolt, rear sight assembly, trigger group and buttplate. U.S. made

barrels can be screwed into a Chinese receiver but not vice-versa. There is no doubt that Polytech and Norinco parts are considerably softer and many will require hardening for safe and proper use. Without expensive rehardening, those parts will wear out quickly. And when they do, they will be difficult to replace as neither the Norinco nor Polytech importers appears maintain an inventory of spare parts in this country.

Norinco also supplied receivers to Century International Arms in the early 1990s. Century used these receivers to build M14-type rifles which were then sold through distribution channels. Century held the Norinco receivers to strict dimensions and standard

Fig. 6-5. Polytech trigger assemblies are well-made. They are marked with a different part number than American military components.

Reproduction Parts

Original M14 parts have become scarce, prompting suppliers to manufacture reproduction parts. Some companies, such as Springfield Inc. have seen to it that their parts meet, if not military specifications, at least their own commercial specifications. And in this country where liability is also a major consideration, commercial specs are often as good as Mil-specs.

Other suppliers have manufactured parts in other countries, including China. Metallurgical tests on many of these parts, hammers in particular, have shown them to be too soft for extended use. Other parts, like the operating rod guide are oversized and require that the stock be relieved before the barreled action can be seated properly. The author has encountered at least one operating rod guide with a hole for the operating rod so large as to be unusable.

National Match rear sights have also been manufactured by a number of different concerns. Some of them are extremely poor, but others are excellent. How can you tell the difference? Study the descriptions of the National Match Rear Sights given in the section of the National Match Rifle and in Appendix B. Check measurements carefully and examine the parts for workmanship. If the measurement are right on, the rear sight assembly will probably be serviceable.

When building an M14-type rifle, it is best to avoid foreign-made parts. Original M14 parts are more expensive and harder to find but will provide far better service in the long run. But how to tell if the part you need is original or a reproduction?

Many parts are investment cast. In this process, a mold is made of the original part and molten metal is poured into the mold under pressure to form the new part. Often, very little is done in the way of heat treating to relieve stress or properly harden the metal. This can be extremely important and even dangerous with parts such as hammers and sears which depend not only on a precision fit, but proper hardness for safe and effective functioning.

It is usually easy to tell if a metal part was investment cast. Look for raised lines or "joins" where the mold parts fit together, for rounded corners and edges — machined parts have sharp, square edges— and machining marks. Investment-cast parts will rarely show machining marks, particularly small parts. Look also for part numbers, inspector's initials or other markings. If they are obscured, shallow, faint or appear abraded, they were molded into the metal and not stamped.

Study Tables 2 and 3 to determine which parts are marked and how. Always look for these markings when buying parts. If you do not see them, the parts are reproductions.

7: TURN YOUR COMMERCIAL M14 INTO A MATCH RIFLE

A custom-built match M14-type rifle capable of less than one minute of angle accuracy at ranges beyond 300 yards can be an expensive proposition, costing from $1,600 to more than $6,500 if ordered from a custom gunsmith (Figure 7-1). But the expense of a custom match rifle can be reduced appreciably if you are willing to work in partnership with an experienced gunsmith. You should know exactly what you want done to the rifle to prepare it for match accuracy. You must also be aware that there are several approaches to converting a standard M14 commercial rifle into a "match quality" rifle. Each has its adherents and detractors. The best way to determine not only what you want done, but which custom gunsmith you would like to have do it, is to attend nearby rifle competitions and question the shooters that perform best. Rare is the rifleman who will not talk at length about "ol' Betsy."

Also, read "The National Match M14," earlier in this text to understand what must be done to prepare an M14-type rifle for match accuracy. A commercial match M14 rifle should, at a minimum, have the following accomplished.

1. Install a National Match barrel, or one which meets National Match standards.

2. Install National Match front and rear sights, or sights which meet National Match standards. Further, as much "gear lash" and side-to-side movement must be removed from the rear sight as possible.

3. "Glass-bed" the stock to fit the receiver

4. Bring the trigger group up to National Match standards

5. Unitize the gas cylinder assembly

6. Select a receiver from a major manufacturer.

Points to Keep in Mind When Ordering A Custom Match M14-type Rifle

After discussions with several custom gunsmiths specializing in building match-grade M14-type rifles, our conversations were summarized best by Fred Johnson of the National Armorer. Fred pointed out that if you expect the rifle to automatically make you shoot better, you are wasting your money. First of all, he said, you must know and practice the basics of shooting — breath control, proper shooting position and so on. Next, don't be misled by the "stories" that are passed around the ranges, i.e., a medium- or heavy-weight barrel will always shoot better than a light or standard weight barrel." Barrel weight does not always affect the accuracy. Rather the care with which the rifling is cut, the muzzle crowned, the chamber dimensioned and the barrel straightened and stress-relieved is far more important. Also, single or double-lugged receivers do not necessarily improve accuracy but they will cause a bedding job to last longer by providing more surface to absorb the recoil forces, but only if the bedding job is properly executed.

Install a National Match Barrel

Unless you are an experienced gunsmith and have the proper tools, jigs and fixtures, do not attempt to install a barrel on an M14 receiver yourself. Leave it to an expert.

Check with the suppliers listed elsewhere in this book for government-produced National Match barrels at what you consider a reasonable cost. If none are available, contact makers of custom barrels for their specifications and prices (See Appendix E). When purchasing either a National Match or a custom-built M14-type match barrel, always request and receive written assurance that the barrel will meet the following National Match specifications.

Barrel does not deviate more than 0° 2' 23" from the centerline.

The muzzle is crowned concentric to the bore at a 90 degree angle and deburred.

Bore diameter is 0.300 + 0.001

Groove diameter is 0.3075 + 0.0010.

Have the new barrel installed on your receiver by a competent gunsmith (Figure 7-2). After installation, the gunsmith should check, and provide you in writing, the following specifications:

Barrel head space, which must fall within the range, 1.6355 to 1.6385 inches.

Barrel and receiver alignment: the flash suppressor/ front sight mount flat at the muzzle end should be parallel with the receiver's horizontal center line. The reading should be as close to zero as possible, and should never exceed 0.003 ± 0.006 inches, otherwise the front sight will not align properly and the gas cylinder may be off-center and change the angle at which the operating rod contacts the bolt, thus preventing consistent lockup.

As important as proper installation is to achieving match grade *reproducible* accuracy, equally important in the M14-type rifle is free-floating the barrel. The barrel should not be supported by, or touch any part of the stock or handguard. It must also not be influenced by sling tautness under any conditions, otherwise, reproducible accuracy will be impossible.

Install National Match Sights

The proper installation of National Match or National Match quality rear and front sights (Figure 7-3) will provide a magnitude increase in accuracy. Be aware that several companies are now offering newly-made National Match Sights. If the sight components meet the specifications listed below, they will provide acceptable service. National Match sight components made under government contract are to be preferred, but are becoming scarce and very expensive.

Fig. 7-1. Geoff Poyer examines a Creedmore Sports custom-built M14 Match rifle in a MacMillan match stock by Gunsmith Jim Gronning.

Fig. 7-2. M14 barrels should always be installed by trained gunsmiths and with the

Rear sight components should be matched to each other and to the receiver for the closest possible fit within the specification.
Receiver: The holes of the windage and elevation knobs should not exceed 0.375 to 0.377 inches I.D. The mounting holes should be centered $6.010 \pm .007$ inches behind the receiver face and $0.188 \pm .004$ inches above the flat rear sight base mounting surface which in turn should be $0.940 \pm .004$ inches above the receiver stock bearing surface.
Elevation Knob Assembly Pinion Shaft bearing surface; 0.372 to 0.370 inches O.D.
Windage Knob Assembly receiver bearing surface; 0.373 to 0.370 inches O.D. The windage knob thread diameter for National Match sights is 0.3125 to 0.3087 inches.
Aperture should fit the sight base as tightly as possible to minimize side-to-side play. This is accomplished by peening and lapping. Discuss this with your gunsmith.

The M14 rear sight aperture is identical to that on the M1 Garand. Aperture specifications are listed in Table 6.
Sight Base: the bearing surfaces of the sight base must be flat in relation to the receiver. The sight base must also allow the sight base to be positioned so that the elevation and windage knob ears are centered.
Sight Cover: the sight cover must fit securely in its slots in the sight base with sufficient spring tension to prevent the sight base from shifting. It must also push down on the aperture enough to keep it flat against, and level with, the top of the receiver.
Detents: The detents on the windage and elevation knobs should be triangular in shape with narrow, straight-edged flats across the tops which mesh with similar detents on the receiver ears, capable of holding position against recoil when proper sight tension is applied. This can be determined by visual inspection to start.

Custom Gunsmith Clint Fowler has developed a clever method for removing the backlash from the M14/M1-type rear sight by installing a small spring which bears on the right ear

Fig. 7-3. National Match rear sights allow adjustments to be made in 1/2 inch Minute of Angle increments.

of the receiver. He also rethreads standard M14/M1-type rear sights from 32 to 64 threads per inch (National Match specifications) by sleeving, thus making it possible to convert a G.I. rear sight to National Match specs at a very reasonable rate. See Appendix E for address and ordering information.

Glass Bedding

Glass-bedding is performed because both wooden and fiberglass stocks have a tendency to compress under stress thus allowing the receiver to move about in the stock. Even the amount of pressure exerted by the trigger assembly on the stock as it holds the receiver in place will cause the wood fibers to compress and the fiberglass stock to wear..

Perhaps the most critical aspect of preparing an M14 rifle, commercial or military, for match quality work involves placing the barreled receiver in the stock in such a way that it 1) is in perfect alignment with the trigger group, 2) does not cause the operating rod to bind and 3) does not allow movement within the stock at any time. There are three ways to accomplish this:

1. Procure a fiberglass stock manufactured for the Ordnance Department. These are available quite inexpensively as surplus items. Select one which provides an exceptionally tight fit and does not allow barreled-receiver movement. The fiberglass stocks will maintain their shape and dimensions somewhat longer than will the walnut or birch stocks. But ultimately, they will also begin to compress under the pounding of recoil (Figure 7-4).

2. Obtain a custom-built match stock from Springfield Armory, MacMillan, Harris, Bishop, etc. See list of suppliers in Appendix E

3. Have your stock glass-bedded. Glass-bedding refers to the technique developed by the Army's Marksmanship Training Unit, of securing the barreled receiver in the stock by seating it in a form-fitting cast of fiberglass. The technique was originally developed for the M1 Garand and later applied to the M14.

Briefly, in the M14 stock, portions of the interior wood surrounding the stock liner are carved away. The area is then filled with a fiberglass or other high-strength polymer compound. The barreled action is inserted into the stock and the fiberglass or polymer is allowed to harden, forming a very tough, form-fitting shroud that holds the barrel in place even under heavy recoil.

A number of different techniques have been worked out for glass-bedding M14-type rifles and each has its adherents and detractors. The newcomer has no real way of judging which of the many techniques is best. A rule of thumb is that the more securely the receiver is held in place, the more accurate the rifle will be, all other factors being equal. At the same time, recognize that the quality of workmanship is also an important factor. Question as many match shooters as possible to find out if they are satisfied with the work of a particular custom gunsmith.

If the reader is proficient with his or her hands, there is no reason why you should not try glass-bedding your own rifle. There are a number of texts that will tell you how to do so (See Bibliography). Perhaps the best discussion of techniques and step-by-step instructions is to be found in Jerry Kuhnhausen's "The U.S. .30 Caliber Gas Operated Service Rifles: A Shop Manual, Volumes I and II" (see Appendix G). Mr. Kuhnhausen discusses the various techniques — basic or pillar — and provides step-by-step instructions to achieve a well-bedded rifle.

Basic glass-bedding instructions are given at the end of this chapter and can be accomplished by anyone handy with tools. It is suggested that before attempting to glass-bed a fa-

Table 6 M14 Rear Sight Aperture Specifications	
Variation	Diameter/Inches
Standard	0.069 - 0.074
Early 1 National Match (no hood)	0.059
Early 2 National Match (no hood)	0.520
Late National Match (hood)	0.595 - 0.5975
Late National Match (hood)	0.0520 - 0.05245

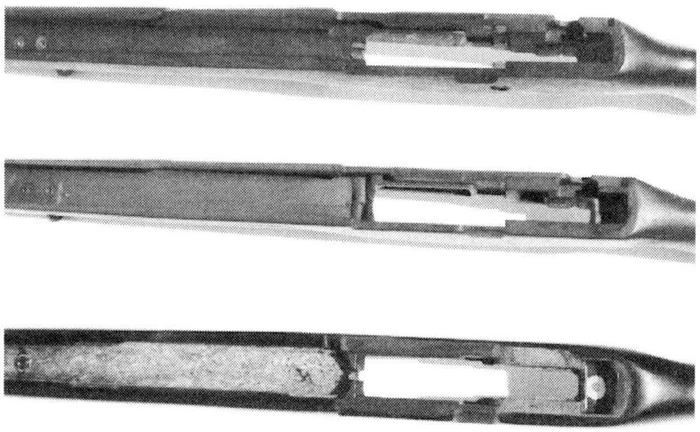

Fig. 7-4. Three variations of M14 stocks compared, from top: standard walnut service; fiberglass service stock; McMillan fiberglass competition stock.

vorite rifle, the reader obtain a spare stock and glass bed a receiver for practice. The glass-bedding technique described below was developed by the Army Marksmanship Unit for the M1 Garand and later applied to the M14. It produces a very close fit between receiver and stock but was designed for a single season's competition, or 2,000 to 4,000 rounds, including practice. Following this technique will not only produce an accurate rifle if accomplished correctly but will provide the shooter with an understanding of the processes involved.

Bring Your Trigger Group to National Match Specifications

The trigger group (Figure 7-5) holds the barreled receiver in the action. It is therefore a critical part of the rifle's operating system which affects accuracy. It must clamp down tightly enough to hold the barreled-action snugly in contact with the stock, yet not so tightly that it tips the receiver downward at the rear or causes the barrel to press against part of the stock.

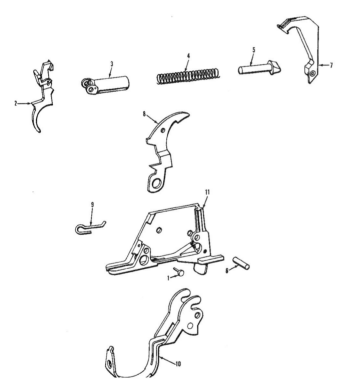

Fig. 7-5. M14-type trigger. 1) Trigger Pin, 2) Trigger/Sear, 3) Hammer Spring Housing, 4) Hammer Spring, 5) Plunger, 6) Hammer Pin, 8) Safety, 9) Safety Spring, 10) Trigger Guard, 11) Trigger Housing.

All elements of the trigger assembly must function smoothly with the least amount of friction possible. And the sear hooks must contact the sear with even pressure to produce a uniform trigger pull.

Begin by disassembling the trigger assembly as described in Appendix D. Examine all parts for wear, rust, pitting or other damage. Check all pin holes to see that the pins are held securely and do not wobble. Check the sear lugs under a strong magnifying glass to see how evenly they contact the sear. Check to make certain that the trigger guard is not bent and that it snaps closed securely. The safety should snap on and off with authority, otherwise the spring must be replaced. Also replace any other parts that appear worn.

Reassemble the trigger and clamp into the rifle. Cock the operating rod and pull the trigger slowly, concentrating on the movement and how it feels. Did you notice any roughness or grittiness in the first stage? Did the second stage let-off occur crisply? Measure the trigger pull with a trigger gauge, or a wire and weights. The minimum allowable military pull for the M14 is 4.5 pounds with 7.5 pounds the maximum. In National Match shooting, the minimum is also 4.5 pounds.

All custom modifications of M14-type trigger assemblies should be left to an experienced gunsmith. Discuss in detail your observations of the present trigger assembly and what he thinks should be done to improve it.

Unitizing the Gas Cylinder Assembly

Unless you are very handy and have at a minimum a drill press at your disposal, this task is best left to an experienced gunsmith. The parts involved, however, are relatively inexpensive and can be replaced if the finished job does not meet expectations. Two methods are commonly used. The US Army procedure required that the gas cylinder assembly be mounted on a jig to make certain that all parts were in direct alignment. Then two holes were drilled through the front band and the

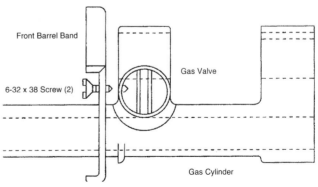

Fig. 7-6. Gas cylinder assembly showing relationship of parts and position of unitizing screws.

valve body, tapped, and held together by two 6-32 x 3/8 inch screws (Figure 7-6).

Some custom gunsmiths tack weld the two components together instead and a bit of controversy rages over the welding method with purists claiming that welding heat will distort the bore of the gas cylinder, thereby restricting gas flow. Jerry Kuhnhausen notes in his definitive text that of the tack welded gas cylinders he has measured, all show some (between 0.001 and 0.002 inches) of bore reduction between the tack welds. On the other hand, many custom gunsmiths will point out that many, many very accurate M14 and M1 Garand match rifles have been built using the tack welding method. Kuhnhausen recommends that if you do use the tack welding method, it be done following the procedure used by US Marine Corps armorers in which the gas cylinder and front band are mounted in a jig and two holes are drilled 0.560 inches apart between the two openings. The band is then TIG welded to the gas cylinder through the holes to keep bore distortion to a minimum. Discuss the pros and cons with your gunsmith.

Selecting Your Receiver

The four commercially-made receivers currently available were discussed in Chapter 5. Make your selection with the information provided in mind.

If you are building a standard grade M14-type rifle, then a standard receiver from any of the four manufacturers will serve you well. Three of the receivers are investment cast, one is milled from bar stock and if you can find one, one was drop forged as were the original military receivers. A note of caution. Avoid original M14 receivers that have been rewelded. 8620 steel does not weld easily and there is always a possibility that a break will occur at the weld with disastrous consequences. And, it is extremely difficult to line up two halves of an original receiver that have been cut with a torch, then reweld them so that all original dimensions are preserved.

If you are building a match grade rifle, you may want to consider spending the extra money to obtain a "lugged" receiver or have lugs attached to your present receiver (Figure 7-7). Lugged receivers are available from all four suppliers of M14-type receivers.

"Lugged" M14-type receivers are of two types, front lugged and rear lugged. The lugs are steel steps welded to the front and/or to the rear of the receiver. These extra bearing surfaces accomplish two things: 1) they provide more surface area for the receiver to bear against the bedding material, thus prolonging the life — and accuracy — of the bedding job. This is especially true of the rear lug. 2) The front lug overcomes the tendency of the receiver to rise up in the stock — bedded or not — during recoil by holding the front of the receiver more securely at that point. The lugs are not only held by the bedding material, but also by bolt through the stock material into the lugs themselves.

Custom gunsmith Clint Fowler points out that the effects of a perfectly bedded, double-legged receiver can be negated by the shooter who overtightens the bolts. He inserts steel bushings through the stock material to prevent this.

Fig. 7-7. Single and double lugged receivers (arrows), such as this double lugged receiver by Armscorp, provide more surface area for secure bedding.

Don't be hung up in your choice of receiver. All four currently available receivers provide excellent service. Be guided by your custom gunsmith if you cannot decide for yourself.

Cryogenic Accurizing

In the past few years, a new technique has been adopted from the machine tool industry that has made tremendous a difference in rifle barrel accuracy. When a rifle barrel is manufactured, it is first turned to close to its final configuration from a steel billet, then drilled for the bore, then reamed and rifled. The gunsmith or manufacturer then turns the barrel to the final shape, threads it, cuts the dovetails or other slots for front sight bases, drills for the gas ports and so on. All of these mechanical operations set up stresses in the barrel that emanate from the sites of such operations and will later interfere with the barrel's natural harmonics. This interference will make itself felt on the bullet as it passes down the tube.

If you view a section of a rifle barrel under a powerful microscope, you will see that the steel is porous. Small black flakes will be scattered here and there and the grain may be uneven. The black specks are really carbon that has precipitated throughout the steel. As you may know, steel is an alloy of iron in which a certain percentage of carbon is distributed. If that distribution is not as even as possible, then the steel will be stronger or weaker depending on where the carbon deposits lie. This in turn will affect the life of the rifle barrel as weaker areas low in carbon will tend to wear out sooner. Areas too high in carbon will be overly hard and may become brittle and cracks will develop.

The process of tempering steel by heating it to certain levels and then allowing it to cool under controlled conditions helps to promote even grain structure and distribute the carbon. But the tempering process has to be done before the machining operations. The application of heat in the tempering after the barrel has been machined to final form affects the steel dimensionally.

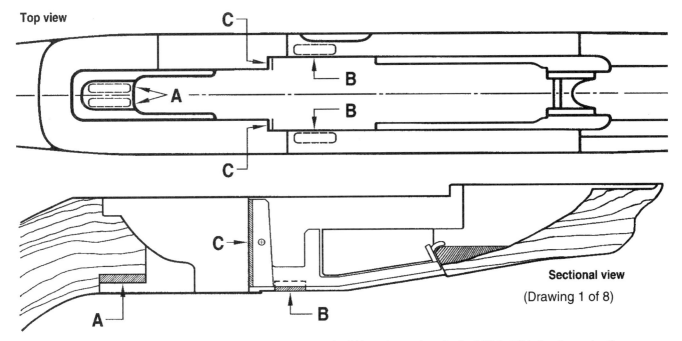

Top view

C

B

B

A

C

Sectional view
(Drawing 1 of 8)

A

B

C

Fig. 7-8. The areas shown by dotted lines and shaded areas should be cut away to a depth of 1/4 to 3/8 inches to receive the bedding compounds. Drawing reprinted with permission of Heritage-VSP Gun Books.

Cryogenic tempering accomplishes stress relief as does heat tempering, but does so without dimensional changes. The barrel is supercooled to temperatures sightly below minus 300 degrees, then allowed to return to room temperature under carefully controlled conditions. The process redistributes the carbon throughout the steel and "smooths" the grain structure. It also relieves all the mechanical stresses set up by the mechanical operations performed on the barrel. The result is a barrel that invariably shoots more accurately and lasts far longer than an untreated barrel.

In discussing the process with Robert Brusan of 300° Below, Inc., he noted that his company has been engaged in cryogenic tempering for many years for the machine tool industry. Varmint shooters concerned with making their barrels last longer first discovered the benefits of cryogenic tempering. "An active varmint shooter can go through a barrel a year," Mr. Brusan pointed out. "After cryo-tempering, not only did their barrels last longer, but reports of greater accuracy started coming back to us."

300° Below, Inc. pioneered cryogenic accurizing for the shooting sports industry through their Accurizing Cryo division. The author has had two rifle barrels cryogenically accurized, an H-S Precision heavy target barrel — fluted — in .308, and a Canadian Arsenals National Match M14 barrel. The results in both cases were extraordinary and resulted in a group sizes that averaged 30% tighter. Neither rifle has been shot sufficiently to determine if an increase in longevity will be seen, but the theory is certainly correct. If for no other reason than increased accuracy, the final touch for a Match M14-type rifle then should be cryogenic accurizing.

But when you choose the facility to do the work, do so with care. It is not as simple as dunking a barrel in liquid nitrogen, as some claim. Too long an immersion in liquid nitrogen, or an improper "warming" period, can lead to excessive brittleness. Stick with those companies who have had long experience in the field, particularly with rifle barrels, and whose equipment is computer controlled.

Glass Bedding an M14-Type Rifle Stock Yourself

Completing a glass-bedding job yourself will not automatically improve accuracy unless the other phases of building a match-quality rifle are accomplished as well. But working through the process will teach you one of the most important techniques involved in the overall process of accurizing an M14-type rifle — or any precision rifle, for that matter. The bedding technique described is relatively easy to accomplish yet will provide excellent support for your barreled receiver. Bedding compound is placed as shown in Figure 7-8 in areas which have been routed out as indicated by the arrows A through C. This drawing from the "U.S. .30 Caliber Gas Operated Service Rifles, Vol. I & II, A Shop Manual," by Jerry Kuhnhausen, is reproduced here by permission of Heritage-VSP Gun Books (See Appendix G).

1. Select a wooden M14 stock, preferably a dark, close grained walnut stock rather than a birch stock. Walnut is slightly denser than birch and will withstand the pounding of recoil better. The fiberglass stocks are more difficult to rout and should be reserved until you have developed the proper techniques.

a. Check the stock with a straight edge to make certain it is not warped.

b. With the proper size spanner wrench, remove the bolt on either side of the stock which secures the stock liner. Remove the stock liner. Do not modify the stock liner in any way for this initial attempt.

c. Using a chisel or a Mototool equipped with a routing bit, cut away wood in the areas shown in Figure 7-8 at the points indicated by arrows A through C, to a depth of 1/8 to 3/16 inches.

d. Work slowly and carefully, keeping all edges as straight as possible. Use a steel straight edge to make the cuts wherever possible.

e. When the cuts have been made, insert the barreled receiver into the stock. Examine it carefully to note where the glass bedding compound must be placed. Mark areas from which the glass bedding compound will run, with a soft lead pencil. Remove the barreled action and using modeling clay, form dams in those areas.

Note: To prevent the barrel from shifting while the bedding compound hardens, make the barrel locating fixture shown in Figure 7-9 from aluminum or brass stock. If made to the exact dimensions shown, it will center the barrel exactly in the forend.

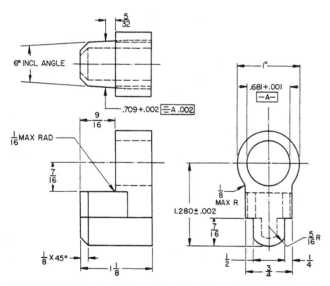

Fig. 7-9. AMU drawing for barrel locating fixture. This fixture is used to hold the barrel in correct alignment in the stock while the bedding materials hardens.

f. Carefully round all sharp edges on the receiver legs so that the receiver can be pulled up and out of the bedding after the polymer sets.

g. Fill all holes, particularly screw holes, with clay to prevent the bedding compound from seeping in under pressure and mechanically locking your receiver into the stock.

h. Chose your bedding material. Brownells offers sev-

eral compounds from which to chose, the most popular being "Acraglas®". Newer compounds offered are "Acraglas Gel®" and Brownells Steel Bed™, a stainless steel-filled epoxy. Rifles have also been glass-bedded successfully with other epoxy compounds which can be obtained from hardware suppliers.

i. Stain and seal the areas of the stock around where the bedding compound will be placed. This will prevent any excess bedding compound from staining the stock. Your routed stock should now look like that shown in Figure 7-10.

j. Now, fill the routed areas with bedding compound. Do not overfill which will squeeze the compound out into unwanted areas and make your cleanup job harder. But at the same time, make certain enough bedding compound is applied to completely support the receiver.

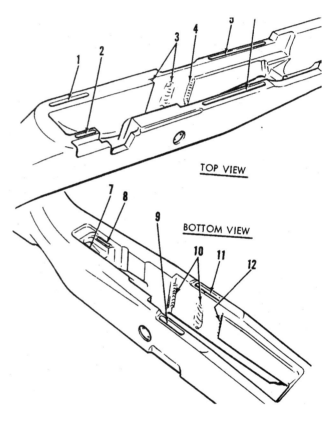

Fig. 7-10. Routed areas (arrows) in the stock should look like those in the drawing.

k. Coat the receiver and barreled action thoroughly with mold release agent. Make certain that no uncoated areas will come in contact with the bedding agent.

l. Insert the barreled action into the stock, seating it down against the stock liners.

m. Insert the trigger guard assembly and close the trigger guard to within 1/4 inch of contact. Use a U-shaped clip made of heavy wire with an opening exactly 1/8 inch wide (Figure 7-11). One leg of the U should go around the front of the trigger guard and the other leg through the hole in the safety. This will position the trigger guard assembly and apply the proper amount of pressure to the barreled action while the bedding compound dries.

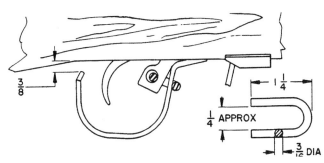

Fig. 7-11. A hook with an opening of 1/4 inch will hold the trigger guard in correct alignment while the bedding hardens. Either make it or procure from Brownells.

n. Make certain the barrel is in the barrel locating fixture and it is centered in the forend.

o. Examine the stock carefully to make certain there are no voids or bubbles in the bedding compound. If so, force more bedding compound in.

p. As soon as the bedding compound has begun to harden and no longer runs, carefully trim away any excess that has squeezed out with an Xacto knife dipped in acetone. Be careful not to cut away too much and jeopardize the support provided by the bedding.

q. When the stock has hardened remove any fixtures or jigs and turn the stock upside down. Support it carefully and using a plastic or wooden mallet and wooden or brass drifts, begin to tap on the underside of the receiver to loosen it and drive it out of the bedded stock (Figure 7-12). Do not strike the bottom of the receiver bridge under any circumstances.

Note: If you have neglected to adequately fill all holes in the receiver legs, or have allowed bedding compound to seep into areas where it should not be, you may find yourself having to work a thin blade down between the receiver and the stock to cut away the excess bedding compound. Of course, this procedure may well negate everything you have accomplished by loosening up the stock again.

r. Once the barreled action is free, you can carefully remove any sharp edges and smooth rough areas with files and sandpaper. Again, be careful not to undercut the support offered by the bedding compound.

s. Finish the stock with a light coat of linseed oil. Or, you might even want to consider applying several coats of polyurethane finish to the inside and outside of the stock to reduce the amount of moisture taken up by the wood as humidity and the seasons change. If so, then remove all old finish from the stock before beginning the bedding process. Use "Simple Green" or a solution of TSP and water to remove as much of the old finish and oil as possible. Scrub the inside and outside of the stock, then dip fine steel wool in acetone and scrub carefully to remove any remaining traces of the original oil finish. Allow to dry thoroughly before beginning the bedding process. After the bedding is completed and thoroughly set, then finish the stock according to the directions on the packaging.

t. You have now finished with the basic bedding procedure for the M14 rifle. When the stock bedding compound and finish has dried completely, you can reseat the barreled action. Do not remove it unless it is absolutely necessary to do so. Removing the action from the bedded stock loosens the metal-to-bedding fit and rounds corners. Many competition shooters remove barreled actions from glass bedded stocks only once a year for a thorough cleaning. Also keep in mind, that no matter how carefully you performed the bedding op-

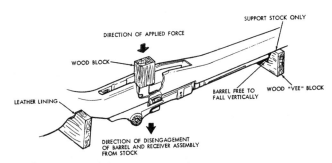

Fig. 7-12. To remove the barreled action from the bedded stock, turn upside down, support under the wrist and tap a hardwood block lightly to move the receiver.

eration, when enough rounds have been fired, the bedding compound will compress allowing the receiver to move. At that point, it will be time to repeat the glass bedding operation on the same, or a new stock. As a rule of thumb, a good bedding job will last nearly half as long as a barrel and then must be redone.

8: TELESCOPIC SIGHTS FOR M14-TYPE RIFLES

The selection of a telescopic sight for an M14-type rifle depends on a number of factors. In the National Matches held under the auspices of either the Director of Civilian Marksmanship or the National Rifle Association, there are two types of shooting venues: first is the service rifle which requires that the M14-type rifle be shot essentially as issued by the military services. No changes are allowed to the exterior of the rifle, including the mounting of telescopic sights. In other types of match rifle competitions, glass bedding and telescopic sights, among other "improvements" are allowed. A complete set of rules governing the conduct of National Match contests can be obtained from the National Rifle Association at 11250 Waples Mill Road, Fairfax, VA 22030-9400 (703 267-3808) or from the Director of Civilian Marksmanship, Civilian Marksmanship Support Detachment, PO Box 576, Bldg 650, Erie Industrial Park, Port Clinton, OH 43452.

Before examining specific telescopic sights, it might be well to take a moment to list some of the considerations to be used in choosing a telescopic sight (Figure 8-1).

Fig. 8-1. Because the M14-type rifle ejects empty cases through the top of the receiver, telescopic sights require a mount offset to the left.

Factors to be Considered

The telescopic sight has two purposes; the first is to brighten the image to make it easier to see at median distances — 50 to 150 yards. The second is to magnify the target at extended ranges. This suggests that the scope's objective lens (front lens) which gathers light, should be as large as possible. Jon Unertl was among the first to realize that a large objective lens produces more accurate shots because the target is brightened and that telescopic tubes did not have to be the same diameter from front to back (Figure 8-2).

Today's telescopic sight has a very large objective lens — at least 30 mm and usually 40 mm. The newest generation of scopes designed for long range and/or precision shooting have objective lenses of 57 mm or larger. These large objectives are especially effective in low light conditions — heavily overcast days, twilight or dawn light.

Fig. 8-2. The Model 1903A4 Sniper Rifle used the Weaver 330 Telescopic Sight (designated the B73B1) which, with its 3/4 inch (19 mm) diameter tube, was typical of pre-WWII scopes.

The next consideration is magnification. It is fashionable to have scopes with huge magnifications — 20 to 30 or more power (written 20x). While they certainly do magnify distant targets, that magnification is accompanied by an ever-increasing amount of shake or jitter. If you are going to be doing the majority of your long range shooting from a steady rest like a shooting bench, then by all means get the most powerful scope you can afford. But if you intend to shoot off-hand or from one of the standard shooting positions, then watch how ever increasing amounts of magnification also increase "target jitter" which is very distracting. And, if you are shooting on a warm day, the highest magnifications will also increase "heat shimmer" or mirage. The longer the distance to the target, the more the heat shimmer will obscure the target.

Perhaps the best solution is a variable power telescopic sight. With a scope of this type you can choose the amount of magnification needed by turning a ring ahead of the eyepiece. Purists will tell you that fixed power scopes are brighter, sharper and last longer than variable power scopes, but with the advances in telescopic sight design and manufacturing over the past four decades, that argument really no longer applies. Keeping in mind the aphorism, you get what you pay for, if you purchase a well-known brand name and pay the price for a precision instrument, that scope should last you for many years. If something does shake lose, all the premium scope manufacturers will repair it for a small fee, if not for free.

Garth Kendig, Technical Representative for Leupold, Inc. and a well-known match shooter in his own right, was consulted for an expert's opinion on telescopic sights, and he added additional factors to be considered when selecting a telescopic sight for long range or matchshooting.

First, the scope should have an adjustment range of 48 to 63 minutes in both elevation and windage. While 48 minutes is adequate on a .308 rifle to reach 1,000 yards, adjusting the scope to an initial 100-yard setting may well eat up 20 to 30 of those minutes.

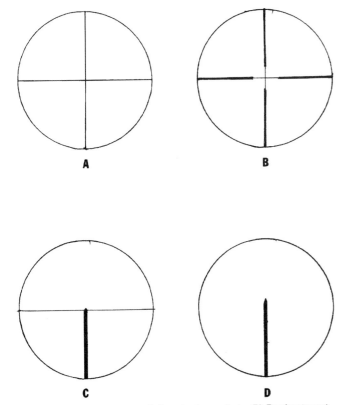

Fig. 8-3. Types of reticles: A) Standard crosshair,, B) Duplex target, C) Crosshair and post and D) post. Both C and D were used in the early M1C Garand M84 and M82 telescopic sights.

The second factor is receiver-to-barrel alignment. Garth pointed out that some receiver/barrel combinations align in such a way that the back end of the receiver tips slightly downward in relation to the barrel, causing the scope to have a slight upward tilt. If this is the case a shim or shims of 0.010 to 0.0150-inch thickness should be used between the rear base and the receiver to bring the scope in line with the bore. The rule is, 0.001 inch under the base will equal one minute of angle on the target.

The third consideration concerns the frequently encountered problem of decreasing elevation adjustment when large amounts of windage are required over long distances. The inside of a telescopic sight resembles a clock. The ideal track for the elevation adjustment is from 6 to 12 o'clock. But as you dial in windage adjustment, you progressively limit the amount of elevation adjustment you can make. For instance, with windage run out near the end of its travel to compensate for strong crosswinds, you will be able to make elevation adjustments only of between 8 and 10 o'clock and this may not be sufficient to reach very long ranges.

The solution is an adjustable windage base. In this way, you rely on the base to accomplish most of the windage adjustment, and preserve the elevation adjustment. You start by centering the internal windage of the scope (run it from end post to end post, counting the clicks, and then dial it back to exactly half that number). Then, with the scope mounted, you sight it in by making initial windage adjustments using the adjustable windage base and moving the rear of the scope in the direction you want the bullet to strike. You should be able to come within a very few minutes of angle using the base windage adjustment only, and finish the last few with the scopes' own internal windage. For the M14-type rifle, the mounting system designed by Brookfield Precision and described below, permits the shooter to make the initial windage adjustment on the base.

The fourth consideration concerns the type of reticle to be used. There are several different styles of reticles, ranging from the standard cross hair to the standing post type used in the M82 scope or the combination cross hair/standing post used in the M84 telescopic sights during World War II and the Korean War (Figure 8-3). Newer, and more effective, are the duplex and mil-dot reticles (Figure 8-4).

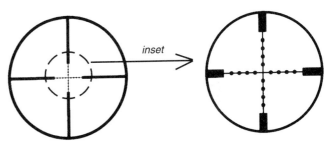

Fig. 8-4. Mil-Dot reticle as developed by Leupold for the USMC and now the standard range estimating reticle for all U.S. Military branches.

The duplex reticle has thick cross wires, extending two-thirds to three-quarters the distance to the center and then narrowing to very thin wires that cross in the center. The mil-dot reticle is similar to the duplex reticle, except that it has eight oval beads each exactly one-quarter mil long, on each cross hair, like beads on a string. A mil (or milliradian) covers exactly 3.6 inches at 100 yards, or 36 inches at 1,000 yards. The mil-dots allow the shooter to judge the range quickly and accurately.

Telescopic Sights

The following telescopic sights have been tested by the author or by a match shooter he respects. All are recommended as rugged and accurate enough for use on M14-type rifles.

Burris. The Burris signature series contains an excellent 4-16x scope with a variety of reticle choices, parallax adjustment, click adjustments and rubber eye guards. While designed for long range hunting, they serve admirably for match shooting when mounted on one of the M14-type mounts described below (Figure 8-5).

Fig. 8-5. Burris 4X-16x Signature Telescopic Sight.

Leupold Vari-X III Tactical Scopes. These scopes were originally developed for FBI sniper use. They are available in 3.5-10x with a 40 or 50 mm objective and 4.5-14x with a 40 mm objective. Duplex or mil-dot reticles are installed and a Leupold rear adjustment mount provides a variable power scope with very good light gathering ability out to 1,000 yards. All have range-finding ability (Figure 8-6).

Fig. 8-6. Leupold's Vari-X Tactical Scopes are extremely popular with law enforcement and precison shooters.

Leupold Mark 3 and Mark 4 Scopes. These fixed power scopes are available in (Mark 3) 6x and 10x and (Mark 4) 10x and 16x. All have built-in elevation adjustment that also serves as a bullet drop compensator. Both the M3 and M4 have an easy-to-use parallax adjustment that can be made from the shooting position.

Springfield Inc. provides two telescopic sights developed for M14-type rifles which use the range-finding principles developed by Captain James Leatherwood. The newest employs a 56 mm objective lens and a 30 mm tube coupled with an internal level which allows the shooter to maintain the vertical and horizontal alignment of the rifle. Magnification is 4x to 14x. A detachable sunshade four inches long can be added and additional shades can be "stacked". This scope is calibrated for the 7.62 mm NATO (.308) cartridge (Figure 8-7).

The government scope model zooms from 6x to 20 power and also employs a 56 mm objective lens. This model is equipped with a mil-dot reticle against which the shooter can calibrate a series of different caliber cartridges.

There are obviously many other telescopic sights that can readily mounted on M14-type rifles than can be tested and described here. If you do not already have a scope in mind, before you invest in one, it might be well to visit several matches and talk with competitors about the scopes they are using. Most shooters will always be glad to talk about their equipment and will not be reticent about pointing out what they consider good or bad features.

Finally, many fine scopes can be mounted on an M14-type rifle and will provide excellent service. As important as the scope is to precision shooting, perhaps even more important is the telescopic sight mounting, as the following paragraphs will demonstrate.

Fig. 8-7. Springfield Inc.'s line of professional telescopic sights grows longer every year. Second generation variable power scopes are available in 4x-14x, 6x x 20x and in fixed 10x. All have 56 mm objective lines.

Scope Mounts

The standard scope mount for the M14-type rifle was developed by the Army Marksmanship Training Unit during the X21 Sniper Rifle development program. The mount is essentially a Weaver base mounted on a piece of steel depending from the left side of the base where it forms a right angle bend

Fig. 8-8. Recoil peens the vertical locating ridge on the original M14 telescopic sight mount, leaving it loose in the vertical locating slot.

and descends for two inches (Refer to Figure 8-1). A hole is drilled near the bottom and a large thumbscrew, held in place by a clip, attaches the scope mount to the side of the receiver via a threaded hole. The inside of the plate has a ridge milled near the bottom which fits into a matching recess in the side of the receiver and a vertical ridge above the thumbscrew which also fits into a matching recess. Both ridges center the mounting plate and keep it from moving. The telescopic sight mounts atop the base with standard one inch Weaver rings. This mount can be removed and when replaced, resumes zero.

The commercial version of this mount is manufactured from high strength aluminum and serves well-enough for 500 to 1,000 rounds. Under the best of conditions, the rifle has to be re-zeroed if the scope is removed and replaced. But the mount ultimately fails for two reasons: first, under recoil, the thumbscrew has a bad habit of backing out, even when the standard clip washer was replaced with a lock washer. And under the repeated impact of recoil, the vertical ridge is peened (Figure 8-8) to the point of uselessness, allowing the scope mount to rock fore and aft, no matter how tightly the thumbscrew is turned down.

If you have one of these mounts and are experiencing this problem, there are two ways to solve it: either buy a new mount or have a gunsmith pin and bolt it to your receiver. Two holes should be drilled for locating pins and two holes drilled and tapped for screws in both the mount and the left side of the receiver to secure the mount. It is suggested that the screws be epoxied into place. The mount remains "semi-removable" but it is securely fastened to the receiver.

An improved variation of this original M14 mount added a set screw to attach the rear of the mount to the cartridge clip guide. This system was used on the M21 Sniper Rifle.

The improved pattern was developed by Brookfield Precision Tool and the Army's 10th Special Forces Group at Fort Devens, MA in the late 1980s. It provides a solid, two-point mounting system: first by retaining the side-mounted thumb screw but including an eccentric cam to add sufficient torque to prevent the thumbscrew from backing out under recoil and second, by eliminating the vertical ridge and using a dovetail to slide into the cartridge guide mount where it is secured in place by a set screw. Set screws near the front of the mount allow the user to enter initial windage and elevation through the base (Figure 8-9).

Fig. 8-9. Brookfield Precision Tool developed a new mounting system in the late 1980s with the Army's 10th Special Forces Group. Armscorp and Smith Enterprises, among others, manufacture an excellent copy.

The original Brookfield M21 mount is available through Creedmore Sports and other suppliers. Similar mounts are manufactured by Armscorp, Entréprise Arms and Smith Enterprises (See Appendix E).

9: NATIONAL MATCH AMMUNITION

The M118 7.62 x 51 mm NATO cartridge was manufactured especially for use in competition and by snipers, and was issued for use in the National Rifle Matches, see Figure 9-1. This round is also known as the .308 Winchester and various ammunition makers have manufactured match grade ammunition to simulate and even improve on the characteristics of the M118 cartridge.

The M118 cartridge has similar performance characteristics to that of the M72 30-06 cartridge developed and manufactured for the M1 Garand National Match rifle. Its uses the same bullet design and its velocity is only slightly less. However, the case length is about one-half inch shorter than that for the M72. The reduced propellant capacity required a different propellant charge from that of the M72 in order to produce a high velocity within a safe pressure level (Figure 9-2).

The M118 round was designed to provide better accuracy than standard issue 7.62 mm military cartridges. Its boat-tail bullet design produces a flatter trajectory and less wind drift. The manufacturing specifications for the match cartridge are significantly more rigid than those for other types of 7.62 mm ball cartridges with respect to accuracy characteristics.

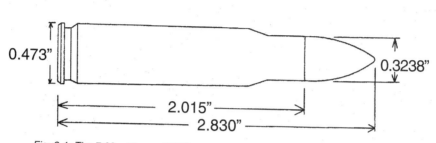

Fig. 9-1. The 7.62 x 51 mm NATO cartridge.

Bullet

The bullet is the completed assembly of a gilding metal jacket and a lead core. The homogenous core material consisting of approximately 90% lead and 10% antimony was purchased in 13" long, 4-7/8" diameter ingots weighing approximately 94 lbs. each. This material was extruded on a 1350 ton hydraulic press into wire having a diameter from 0.223 to 0.226 inch. The wire was fed from reels into a machine which formed lead slugs weighing 115.0 + 0.2 grains at a rate of 9600 pieces per

Fig. 9-2. The 7.62 x 51 mm NATO M118 round on the right is a reduced version of the M72 .30-06 (7.62 x 54 mm) cartridge on the left.

hour (Figure 9-3).

The bullet jacket was drawn and formed from a metal cup consisting of 90% copper and 10% zinc. This cup was manufactured to specific dimensions and tight tolerances. The jacket was formed from these special cups in two draw operations and was trimmed within a 0.005 inch tolerance to maintain a jacket weight ranging between 58.5 and 60.0 grains.

The trimmed jacket and formed slugs were then assembled on a 14 station, 35 ton capacity press having a production rate of 2800 pieces per hour. The finished bullet had a length ranging from 1.312 - .040 inches and a diameter of 0.3081 to 0.3088 inch and a maximum point diameter of 0.060 inch. The profile had a radius of 2.1 inches and a boat tail length 0.230 - .005 inch. The bullets were visually inspected prior to assembly into cartridges. Bullets passed through a weighing machine which had three stations. Bullets with a weight between 172.6 and 174.5 grains were taken off at station 2. Bullets lighter than 172.6 grains were taken off at station 1 and scrapped. Bullets heavier than 174.5 grains were collected at station 3 and given separate control numbers. The bullets were then inspected visually as they rotated on a chain conveyor with a mirror beneath so that the entire surface area of the bullet could be seen.

Case

The case serves several purposes. It secures the bullet, primer and propellant to form one unit; it acts as a cam to guide the cartridge from the magazine into the chamber; and it also acts as an obturator to prevent gas from escaping back into the rifle mechanism.

The case was formed from a cup through a series of punch and die draws and annealing operations. The cup was made from brass (70 percent copper and 30 percent zinc) and had to meet weight and grain size requirements. The finished M118 case had a length of 2.015 - .015 inches, a head diameter of 0.473 - .007 inch, an inside neck diameter of 0.3068 + .0010 inch, an outside diameter of 0.3238 inches and a neck wall thickness of 0.017 - .004 inch.

The case head was shaped by smashing it between a punch and die and then smashing it again to form the primer pocket and imprint the letters and numerals in the head. The two heading operations hardened the brass around the primer to prevent gas leakage and head ruptures during firing. The case was heat treated to obtain a certain grain size and hardness in the varying wall thickness to give good obturation and extraction characteristics. The case wall thickness was greater at the rear because a portion of the case is unsupported by the chamber or bolt at this point.

The front of the case had a smaller wall thickness and it was softer so that it expands against the chamber to prevent gas escaping into the weapon. A primer pocket and a vent hole were formed in the base of the case and an extractor groove was cut into the side of the case just forward of the base. In the final operation the vent hole was pierced and the primer was assembled in the primer pocket. A

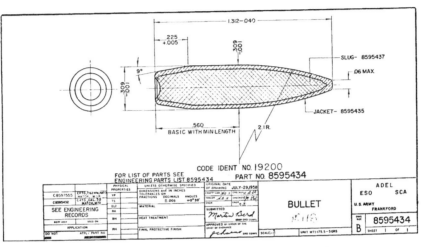

Fig. 9-3. Frankford Arsenal drawing of the M118 7.62 mm boat-tail bullet.

waterproofing material was applied between the primer and case at the same time. Automatic devices detected cases with no vent hole or an eccentric vent hole, and cases with no primer or an inverted primer. The completed cases were also visually inspected.

Primer

The primer used in the M118 cartridge was an assembly consisting of a cup, pellet, and anvil. Also, a paper disc was sometimes inserted between the anvil and pellet. The cup was formed from annealed-cartridge-brass strip with a thickness of 0.0290 + .0005 inch. The finished cup had a diameter of 0.2106 - .0011 inch and a minimum thickness of 0.028 inch at the base.

The pellet was assembled in the cup while it was in the plastic state. The pellet was formed by means of a charging plate which had 1,020 holes. The pellet diameter was 0.1375 + .001 inch and it was 0.077 - .001 inch thick. The primer mix was rubbed into the holes in the plate. Pellet samples were taken from the production line periodically and weighed to assure a dry weight of 0.500 + .08 grains.

The anvil was formed from rolled and tempered cartridge brass. It had a height of 0.086 - .0025 inch and a diameter of 0.1844 - .0005 inch. The anvil was pushed into the pellet in the cup and the primers were placed in an oven at 120°F to dry the moisture from the pellet after which they are stored at 90-100°F prior to priming.

Propellant

The propellant used in match cartridges had to meet a number of requirements. In addition to giving the bullet a particular velocity level with a safe pressure, it had to provide satisfactory performance at extremes of temperatures and produce a minimum of smoke, flash, fouling and barrel erosion. The propellant used in the M118 round gives the bullet a velocity of 2550 + 30 feet per second at 78 feet from the muzzle when fired in a 22-inch test barrel. The length of test barrel simulated that used in the M14 rifle.

A limit was imposed on the variation in velocity from shot to shot since long range accuracy is dependent on both the basic dispersion such as that obtained at short range and the velocity variation. The specification required that the standard deviation of velocities not exceed 28 feet per second. The average chamber pressure limit was 50,000 pounds per square inch. To assure functioning in the M14 rifle, a further requirement of the propellant used in the M118 round was that the port pressure had to be 12,500 + 2000 psi. The appropriate charge of propellant was established by means of velocity tests.

Samples of loaded cartridges were taken from the production line twice daily and fired in a test rifle for velocity to maintain the desired velocity level. The ammunition was conditioned to a temperature of 70 + 2 degrees F before firing velocity tests.

Cartridge Assembly

The primed case, propellant and bullet were assembled into a cartridge on a multiple-station press which produced 2,000 cartridges per hour. The overall length of the M118 was 2.830 ± .030 inches. The cartridges were gaged and weighed on a seven-station automatic machine which checked the profile and alignment, the head to shoulder length, the total length, the diameter of the extractor groove, the depth of the primer, the diameter of the head, the thickness of the head, and the cartridge weight. Cartridges which failed to meet the dimensions established were rejected. The cartridges were all visually examined.

Testing

During production of the match cartridges, the bullets and cartridges were subjected to daily quality control accuracy tests. This firing was conducted on a 600 yard outdoor range in an accuracy test rifle consisting of an M1919A4-machine-gun-type barrel and an M1903 rifle action. The barrel was secured in a slide which operated in a V block attached to a Frankford Arsenal Machine Rest. The barrel length for the rifle firing the M118 round was 22 inches. The acceptance

determined and this measurement was entered on the tarage table to obtain a corresponding pressure in pounds/square inch. Since the load applied to the cylinder in developing the tarage table was a static one and that applied when the round was fired was dynamic, this calculated result was not a true pressure reading. However, this system did provide an adequate measure of the safety of the cartridge.

Cartridge samples were further tested in a National Match rifle to assure proper functioning.

A bullet pull test was conducted to assure that the bullet would remain secure in the case during insertion and removal from the rifle. The requirement was a bullet-pull force of not less than 20 pounds.

Table 7
.308/7.62 mm NATO Ballistic Performance

| | | Velocity in Feet per second | | | | Mid-Range Trajectory | | | | |
| | | | Yards | | | | | | | |
Cartridge	Wt/Grs	Muzzle	100	200	300	100	250	300	400	500
.308 Win	150	2860	2520	2210	1930	+3.7	0	-4.5	-20	-47.5
.308 Win	180	2616	2250	1940	1680	+3.0	0	—	-38	—
.308 Win	200	2450	2210	1980	1770	+3.0	0	-12.0	-35	-48.5

test requirement was a mean radius of 3.5 inches for nine 10-shot groups from each of three test rifles at a range of 600 yards. The mean radius represented the average distance of each shot in the group from the group center.

The velocity was calculated at a distance of 78 feet from the muzzle by measuring the time required for the bullet to pass over a known distance. Photoelectric screens were used to detect the passage of the bullet and signals were fed into a chronograph to start and stop the counting mechanism. The photoelectric screens were positioned at distances of 28 and 128 feet from the rifle muzzle to give a base distance of 100 feet. The velocity was then calculated from the formula, v = 100/t.

The maximum chamber pressure was calculated by means of copper crusher cylinders. The crusher cylinders had a length of 0.4010 - .0020 inch and a diameter of 0.2265 - .0020 inch. Sample cylinders were subjected to a static load and their change in length was determined leading to the development of a tarage table. The pressure gage consisted of a test barrel with standard chamber and bore dimensions on which a hole was drilled through the chamber wall to accept a steel piston. A yoke permitted a crusher cylinder to be positioned between the piston and a threaded anvil so that the cylinder was compressed on firing. The change in length of the cylinder was

Ballistic Performance

In addition to accuracy performance, the shooter is interested in elevation and wind drift requirements. The author conducted tests using an M14-type rifle built on an Entréprise receiver with a National Match barrel by Canadian Arsenals, described elsewhere in this book and an Oheler Chronograph. The data presented in Table 7 shows the elevation characteristics for this particular rifle. Keep in mind that elevation and windage requirements will vary somewhat from rifle to rifle because of variations in velocity level. Muzzle velocities were measured at 20 feet to eliminate muzzle blast interference; velocities for the 100, 200 and 300 yard measurements were taken from manufacturer's data for the cartridges used. Those interested in obtaining the most from their match rifles should repeat these tests for their favorite rifle/ammunition combinations.

Calculating wind drift is as much an art as a science. Use the information presented in the Table 8 to help you estimate wind velocity and its effects on a bullet passing down range. First, memorize the identifying factors that allow you to estimate wind velocity, then build a table like that shown in Table 9 for your own rifle/ammunition combination. Any high power shooter will tell you that more matches are won and lost on the same distance in a vacuum. While somewhat complicated, General Hatcher developed the following table (Table 9) for the 172 grain M1 boat tail bullet, it serves well enough as a starting point for estimating wind drift for the M118 boat tail, 172 grain bullet.

From this table, it can be seen that a bullet fired at a target 600 yards distant with a 7 mile an hour wind blowing at right angle to the bullet's line of travel will cause it to be deflected 18.2 inches, while that same bullet fired at a target 900 yards distant will be deflected 47.18 inches.

The author prefers to record this data in the "Champion Rifle National Match Course Score Book" by E.F. (Tod) Sloan, Colonel, USA, Ret, who was a former Distinguished Rifle Marksman and National Rifle Champion in 1931. The booklet includes a series of windage diagrams which are very clear and concise — and easy to memorize — and which the shooter can modify to suit his particular rifle/ammunition combination. By carefully filling out the "score sheet" for each shooting session, you quickly establish a data base from which to draw conclusions applicable to wind/lighting/rifle/ammunition conditions (See Figure 9-4).

Obtaining the Highest Level of Performance from the Ammunition

The following two tips will assist the shooter in obtaining the highest level of performance from his or her M14-type rifle and ammunition.

1. Use the M118 match cartridge, or its civilian equivalents, only in chambers designed for the 7.62mm NATO or .308 Winchester cartridge.

correct estimation of wind drift than any other factor.

More than seventy years ago, Julian S. Hatcher, Major General, USA, Ret, who had led a long and distinguished career in the US Army Ordnance Corp and was a well known match shooter in his own right, developed a formula for calculating wind drift in which $D = W (T-T_v)$ where D is deflection caused by wind, W is wind velocity across the range in feet per second, T is the time of flights in seconds across the range and T_v is the time it would take the same bullet to traverse

---

Table 9
Wind Deflection of a 172 Grain Boat tail Bullet
Initial Velocity 2,700 fps

Range/Yards	Time of Flight	Time of Flight in a vacuum	Difference	Deflection in inches	Deflection in feet
100	.115	.111	.004	.006	.07
200	.237	.222	.015	.022	.26
300	.367	.333	.034	.050	.60
400	.506	.444	.062	.091	1.09
500	.665	.555	.100	.147	1.76
600	.815	.667	.148	.217	2.60
700	.989	.778	.211	.309	3.71
800	1.117	.889	.288	.422	5.06
900	1.383	1.000	.383	.562	6.74
1,000	1.608	1.111	.497	.729	8.75

---

2. The velocity of the bullet increases with an increase in temperature. Therefore, try to maintain a uniform ammunition temperature during firing by avoiding direct exposure of the rounds to the sun for extended periods, and by maintaining a uniform firing rate so that a cartridge is not heated excessively while in the chamber.

Table 10
National Match Ammunition Ballistic Requirements
7.62mm M118
2550 ± 30 feet/second
Pressure - Not to exceed 50,000 lbs./square inch
Accuracy - 3.50 inch Mean Radius Maximum Average

Commercial .308 Ammunition

The .308 Winchester was developed by Winchester in 1952 as a hunting round and adopted by the military in 1954 (Figure 9-5). The M14 rifle was chambered for the .308 round, designated the 7.62 X 51 mm NATO cartridge which has slightly different dimensions than the commercial .308.

The gas-operated M14 handles ammunition in a rough manner from the time it is stripped from the magazine, through

being slammed into the breech by the bolt face, hard enough to set the shoulder back .001+, through extraction when the still slightly expanded cartridge is yanked from the chamber. This stresses the brass in the area of the web and unless reinforced, case head separations occur. Frankford Arsenal solved this problem by increasing the thickness of the brass in the case by adding nearly 25 grains more metal. This means, among other things, that a military case will hold sightly less powder than a commercial case. It also means that commercial .308 cartridge cases should not be used in M14-type rifles unless they have reinforced heads.

Fig. 9-5. M118 Match, (l) was designed expressly for use in the M14 to increase accuracy. Federal's Gold Medal .308 provides similar accuracy and is more easily obtainable.

Reloading for the M14-Type Rifle

If you are a novice reloader, *don't*. First, gain a great deal of experience before reloading for any gas-operated military rifle. For gas-operated military rifles to operate reliably requires a

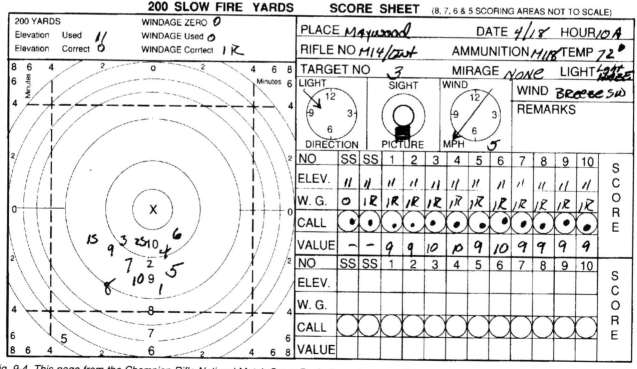

Fig. 9-4. This page from the Champion Rifle National Match Score Book shows how easy it is to compile a personal data base — providing that you complete it carefully during each shooting session.

cooperative partnership between the rifle manufacturer and the ammunition manufacturer in the way of very strict specifications for both. If your handloads do not meet the specifications set for the rifle/ammunition combination, you are playing with fire — or in this case, a bomb.

If you are an experienced handloader, study the description of the M14 match ammunition manufacturing process given above and note where it is imperative that you hold yourself to very strict standards. Many experts on the M14 flatly state that you should not reload commercial cases for the M14. The author suggests that you would be wise to listen to them. But if you absolutely must reload, then study the descriptions of military loads in reloading manuals very carefully and use either the M118 case or Gold Medal .308 match case as manufactured by Federal Cartridge Company. It has thicker case walls, although still not to military specs. Check with the manufacturer of other brands of cases before reloading them.

You can also use once-fired non-match military brass from any American manufacturer — most foreign manufacturers will meet NATO specification but they use Berdan primers and these are almost impossible to remove from military casings. Reloading into these is simply is not worth the effort.

No specific reloading data is given in this book. The subject requires the presentation of far more information than can be given here.

Perspectives on the 7.62 mm NATO Cartridge

The 7.62 mm NATO/.308 Winchester is essentially a downsized version of the .30-06. However, when loaded with a 150 grain bullet, there is only a 5 grain powder difference which translates to a loss of only about 100 fps in velocity in the .308 over the .30-06.

The 168 grain Match King bullet by Sierra has long been considered the ultimate bullet where accuracy is concerned

for the .308. Virtually every sniper and high power match cartridge in .308 is loaded with this bullet. In a recent experiment, the author fired ten rounds loaded with the 168 grain Match King and ten rounds of Sierra's 172 grain spire point, boat-tail base bullets at 100 yards from an M14-type match rifle. The 168 grain bullet group was 0.475 inches in diameter, that for the 172 grain bullet was 0.985 inches. Perhaps the most popular .308 cartridge for long range precision shooting is the Federal Gold Medal .308 Winchester Match Cartridge. Loaded with a 168 grain bullet, this cartridge has established standards of excellence that are hard to beat.

Out to 600 yards, the service .308 cartridge matches that of the .30-06 M2 or AP in accuracy. Beyond 600 yards, the .30-06 cartridge holds a slight edge. The 7.62 NATO round has a mean velocity of 2,860 fps and a mean energy of 2,730 foot pounds when loaded with the 150 grain bullet.

The M14/M1A performs wonderfully well in the 800-1,000 yard range; some say better even than the M1 Garand. But you have to select the right ammunition, or if experienced, reload for it. The 172 grain bullet in the M118 is marginal for these extended ranges but since the first edition of this book, a number of new bullet weights and designs have appeared. The author's experience with them is still limited but their ancestry leaves little doubt of what their effectiveness will be.

The author has tested Hornady's new A-Max bullets in 175 and 178 grains, Berger's new 185 VLD (Very Low Drag) and Hornady's 185 and 190 grain Match bullets. All have performed very well and provided sub-minute of angle groups at both 800 and 1,000 yards through the the author's long range M14-type rifle built by Jim Gronning of Grüning Precision, and described in Chapter 5. Not enough testing has been accomplished at this point to declare preferences.

10: OPERATING INSTRUCTIONS

References to select fire assemblies are included for documentary purposes only. When operating your semiautomatic M14-type rifle, disregard all references to the select fire mechanisms.

An overall view of the M14-type rifle is shown in Figure 10-1. 1) Buttplate; 2) Stock, 3) Trigger Assembly, 4) Rear Sights, 5) Operating Rod, 6) Handguard, 7) Barrel, 8) Front Sight Assembly, 9) Flashhider, 10) Bayonet Lug, 11) Gas Plug, 12) Gas Assembly, 13) Gas (Spindle) Valve, 14) Front Barrel Band, 15) Forend, 16) Front Sling Swivel, 17) Magazine, 18) Magazine Release, 19) Pistol Grip, 20) Stock Bolt, 21) Rear Sling Swivel, 22) Sling.

Rifle Controls

Selector. The selector switch is located on the right side of the receiver just below the rear sight. Its function is to change the firing mode of the rifle between semiautomatic and automatic. When the selector is turned with its blank face toward the rear and the ear type projection downward, the rifle will fire semiautomatically. When the selector is positioned with face marked "A" toward the rear and the ear type projection upward, the rifle will fire automatically.

Commercial M14-type rifles lack the selector switch assembly.

Trigger and Sear Assembly. The trigger and sear assembly is located inside the trigger guard assembly and is part of the firing mechanism (Figure 10-2). It functions to control the firing of the rifle in both semiautomatic and automatic modes.

When firing the rifle in the semiautomatic mode, squeeze the trigger once for each round fired.

When firing in the automatic mode, squeeze trigger and hold.

Safety. The safety is located on the firing mechanism near the guard assembly. Its function is to block the trigger and sear and lock the hammer to keep the rifle from firing. To fire, press the safety forward. The rifle has to be cocked for the safety to function.

Gas Valve System. The gas or gas spindle valve (Figure 10-3) is located at the front of the stock and is connected to the gas cylinder. Its function is to control the gases generated by the fired cartridge to operate the rifle. When the slot on gas valve is in the vertical or "ON" position, the gas valve is open, releasing the gases from the bore into the gas cylinder.

When gas valve slot is in the horizontal or "OFF" position, the gas valve is closed, shutting off the release of gas from the bore. This permits all of the gas to be used to propel the rifle grenade. If you plan to use your rifle in competition, consider having the gas valve tack welded or dimpled in the "ON" position permanently. More than one shooter's score has taken a nose dive when the gas valve was inadvertently turned to the "OFF" position.

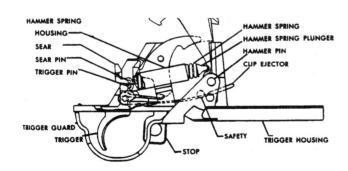

Fig. 10-2. Trigger Guard Assembly.

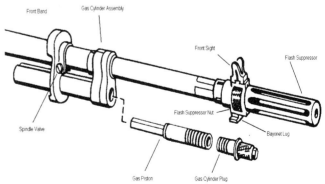

Fig. 10-3. Gas Valve System.

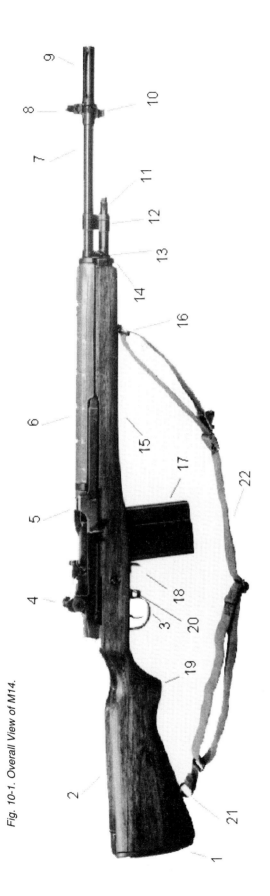

Fig. 10-1. Overall View of M14.

Rear Sight Controls

The controls for the rear sight assembly are shown in Figure 10-4.

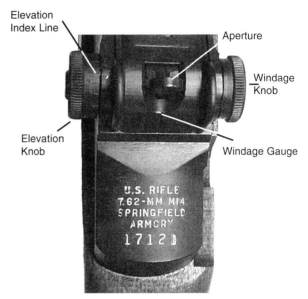

Fig. 10-4. Rear Sight Assembly.

Windage knob. The windage knob is located at the right rear side of the receiver. Its function is to adjust the sideways or lateral movement of the rear sight.

To move the sight to the *right*, turn the windage knob *clockwise*. To move it to the left, turn windage knob *counterclockwise*.

Pinion assembly. The pinion assembly (elevation knob) is located at the left rear side of the receiver and is calibrated in meters. Its function is to adjust the *up* and *down* movement, or elevation, of the aperture, i.e., turn pinion *clockwise* to *raise*; *counterclockwise* to *lower*.

Operating Rod Handle

The operating rod handle (Figure 10-5) is located on the right-side of receiver. To cock the rifle, move operating rod handle to the rear position and release. The magazine spring forces a new cartridge in the magazine to the top where it is held by the magazine lips. The bolt, as it moves forward when the operating rod is released, pushes against the base of the cartridge ramming it forward into the breech.

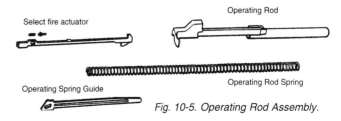

Fig. 10-5. Operating Rod Assembly.

Bolt Assembly

The bolt assembly (Fig. 10-6) consists of the extractor, ejector spring and plunger, extractor spring, firing pin, bolt body and roller assembly. The bolt is connected to the operating rod handle via the recess in which the bolt roller enters. The firing pin is cocked by the sear when the operating handle is moved to the rear.

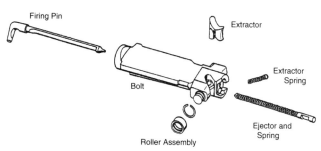

Fig. 10-6. Bolt Assembly

Bipod Controls

Jaw, Self-locking Bolt. Using the combination tool, tighten the self-locking bolt in right jaw. This clamps both jaws to the gas cylinder. To remove, use the combination tool to loosen the self-locking bolt in the right jaw. Spread the jaws and remove bipod from rifle.

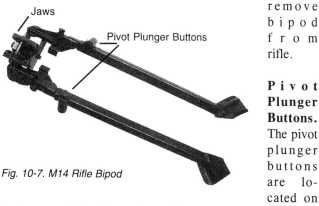

Fig. 10-7. M14 Rifle Bipod

Pivot Plunger Buttons. The pivot plunger buttons are located on the leg assemblies. Press the top button on either leg to rotate the leg to an open or closed position. Press the bottom button on either leg to extend or close the leg, see Figure 10-7.

Operating the M14 Rifle Under Normal Conditions

Preparing to Fire. Examine the bore to be sure it is free of powder fouling or corrosion. Check the gas cylinder plug to make certain it is secure. Check your ammunition to make certain it is clean and of the correct caliber. If you are using the bipod, make certain it is mounted correctly and the legs are secured.

Loading. Insert the front end of a loaded magazine into the magazine well until the front catch snaps into engagement; then pull rearward and upward until the magazine latch locks the magazine into position. If the magazine is empty, once in place, it can be loaded using 5-round clips, or by inserting one cartridge at a time.

To do so, press the safety backward to the "ON" position. Draw the operating handle all the way to the rear, depress the bolt lock and ease bolt forward until it is stopped by the bolt lock. Place a loaded clip into the clip guide slot and push it down until bottom of the clip touches top of magazine follower. With the fingers of the right hand under the housing of the firing mechanism and the ball of the thumb on the body of the top cartridge near the clip, press cartridges straight down into the magazine. Withdraw the clip, replace with a loaded clip and repeat the operation until the desired number of rounds to twenty, have been loaded.

An alternate method uses the combination tool. Insert the cartridge clip in cartridge clip guide. Place the open end of the tool on the base of the cartridge at the top of the clip. Push downward, forcing cartridges into magazine.

To close the bolt, remove the clip from the guide, release the bolt lock by drawing bolt rearward and letting it go forward.

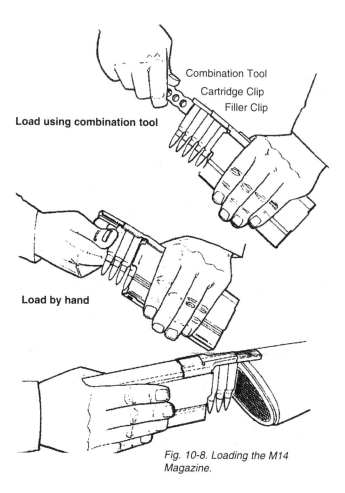

Fig. 10-8. Loading the M14 Magazine.

Release the safety to fire.

To load the magazine when removed from the rifle, install the filler clip, if available, on the top rear of the magazine, see Figure 10-8. Insert the cartridge clip into filler and force cartridges into magazine using the combination tool, your fingers or by placing the top cartridge against rifle's butt plate and forcing the cartridges into magazine. If no clip is available, lay each cartridge on the magazine follower plate and press down to slide the cartridge below the magazine lips. Make certain that the bullet tip clears the top of the magazine's front wall.

Firing

Note: The commercial, non-military M14-type rifle and all after-market M14-type receivers are not capable of full automatic fire. They are manufactured without provision for the selector switch assembly. To fire these rifles, follow the instructions given below, ignoring any that deal with the selector switch assembly.

Set the safety to "ON" by pulling it back. Insert the magazine. Pull the operating handle to the rear and let it go forward under its own spring power to chamber a round.

Semiautomatic only. Push the safety "OFF," pull the trigger to the rear to fire each round.

Semiautomatic Fire with Selector Shaft Lock. On rifles containing the selector shaft lock, push the safety forward. With each squeeze of the trigger the rifle will fire one round.

Semiautomatic Fire with Selector. With the selector shaft lock removed and the selector installed, position the selector for semiautomatic fire. Push the safety forward and with each squeeze of the trigger the rifle will fire one round.

Automatic Fire With Selector. Position selector for automatic fire. Push the safety forward. Squeeze the trigger and the rifle will fire automatically as long as trigger is held back and there is ammunition in the magazine. Release trigger to stop firing.

Note: After the last round is fired, the magazine follower actuates the bolt lock to retain the bolt in the rearward position. After inserting a loaded magazine and with the muzzle pointed in a safe direction, either depress the bolt lock on the left side of the receiver to let the bolt go forward and chamber a new round, or pull the bolt handle back to unlatch the bolt and let it go forward. A third method involves placing the edge of your right hand against the bolt handle to hold it back while depressing the magazine follower with your thumb. As soon as the bolt starts to move forward, remove your hand from the bolt handle, letting it snap forward. Do not control the bolt while it is moving forward or the cartridge may jam.

Unloading

a.   Push the safety to the "ON" position.

b.   Grasp the magazine with your fingers, placing the thumb on the magazine latch, and squeeze. Push the magazine forward and downward to disengage it from the front catch and remove the magazine from the magazine well.

c.   Pull the operating rod handle to the rear to extract and eject the chambered round. *Inspect the chamber, making certain the rifle is clear.*

Weapon's Check Procedures

Before shooting the rifle, perform the checks listed in Table 10.

Table 10
Weapons Check: Before Firing

1. Clean chamber, bore and all components and lubricate except for the gas cylinder and piston

2. Wipe rifle's exterior surface to remove excess oil

3. Check gas cylinder plug to make certain it is tight (do not tighten when weapon is hot)

4. Work the operating rod and bolt. They should function smoothly without binding

5. Safety Mechanism: move the safety ON and OFF

6. Rear Sight: turn windage knob and pinion assembly five clicks in either direction to make certain they move smoothly

7. If using the bipod, check yoke jaws for smooth functioning and a secure hold on the rifle. Clean and lubricate as needed

---

Table 11
Zeroing the M14

To zero the M14 or M14-type rifle, follow these six steps:

(1) Raise aperture from lowest position by eight clicks elevation—turn the knob on the left side of the receiver counter-clockwise 8 clicks.

(2) Align the windage center index line on sight base with center index line on receiver.

(3) Fire three warmup rounds.

(4) Fire four additional rounds at a target. Adjust the sights after each round to move point of impact to center of target. If the bullet strike is high on the target, adjust the knob down one click and fire another shot. If the bullet strike is low on the target, adjust the knob up one click and fire another shot.

Then fire five consecutive rounds semiautomatically. The impact of the 5-round shot group should be within a 6.1-inch diameter circle.

(4) Adjust sights to bring point of impact of round to center of target by correcting with one click of elevation or windage for each 28 millimeters (approx. 1-1/8 in.) of movement required.

(5) Maximum adjustments permitted are: six clicks elevation or depression and/or three clicks windage in either direction.

(6) After the rifle has been zeroed, loosen the locking screw on the pinion assembly which secures the elevation knob. Turn the elevation knob until the 100-meter mark (between "2" and "12") is aligned with mark on the side of receiver. Tighten the screw to lock the knob.

11: SHOOTING THE M14-TYPE RIFLE

There are four basic positions for shooting the M14 rifle: standing, kneeling, sitting and prone. A fifth position, bench resting, is used for sighting in and testing ammunition loads. Standing is the least steady position, kneeling is the next steadiest and prone provides excellent support if executed correctly. Bench resting is the steadiest of all as the gun is fully supported.

Clothing

Wear a soft cotton tee shirt to prevent chafing. Over that don a middle-weight sweat shirt for cushioning. The shooting jacket should be buckled tightly over the sweat shirt. Pants should be loose enough to allow you to kneel and stand without binding — expanded fit jeans are ideal — as are military utilities and sweat pants. Wear wool socks that absorb moisture and comfortable shoes that will provide a stable platform. Cross-trainer athletic shoes are ideal.

Positions

Standing

In match shooting, the standing position (Figure 11-1) is perhaps the most important as this is more difficult to master than the kneeling or the prone where everyone shoots better and best. When standing, you are balanced on two legs and are holding a heavy object perpendicular to the spine. Gravity becomes your worst enemy and is aided and abetted by your body's autonomic movements — heart and pulse rates and muscle tremors.

To shoot well from a standing position, hold the rifle steady and squeeze the trigger so as not to disturb the point of aim. Easy to say, hard to do. Practice and concentration

Fig. 11-1. Standing position.

are the keys which will allow you to progress from consistent eight ring to nine ring to ten ring scores over time.

Stand so that you are facing 90 degrees from the target, feet comfortably planted slightly less than your shoulder's width and with the weight distributed evenly on both feet. Keep your legs straight but do not lock your knees. Keep your hips level and in line with your shoulders. From the hips up, turn your spine slightly to the left so that your shoulders turn toward the target. Do not thrust your hips out. The pain you feel will gradually disappear as your back muscles strengthen. Let your left arm carry the rifle's weight by resting your elbow on your rib cage — bone-to-bone support. A properly adjusted sling will enhance this position. The left wrist should be straight and allow the hand to assume a natural bend as it cradles the forend. The head should be held erect with the eyes looking straight ahead through the sights to the target. Adjust your feet placement until you achieve this line. The right elbow can be carried high or low as the shooter wants but it should place the right hand comfortably around the pistol grip so that the ball of the index finger rests on the trigger. Pull the rifle tight against your shoulder and cheek, take a breath, let half out and achieve your sight picture, then squeeze the trigger.

Kneeling

The most popular kneeling position is the "High Kneeling" in which the back is kept relatively straight and the overall position is erect. The forward and low positions allow the shooter to bend the spine so that he or she is leaning forward. Your choice of either

Fig 11-2. High kneeling position.

should determined solely on what works best for you. Test each position over several shooting sessions and compare your average scores from each.

High Kneeling: Position the sling and turn 45 or so degrees from the target (Figure 11-2). Place your right knee on the mat at about 60 degrees from the target with the ankle resting on a "kneeling roll" or rolled up beach towel or other soft support. The heel should be in contact with the base of the spine. This allows the foot and kneeling roll to bear three-quarter's of the body's weight.

The left leg faces nearly in line with the target with the lower part of the leg vertical and the left thigh almost in line with the left forearm. Now place the left elbow joint just past the front of the knee so that the bone of the upper arm is pressed down on the knee. The sling should be supporting the rifle's weight while it rests on the heel of the left hand. Do not grasp the rifle with your fingers, but keep them straight along the sides of the forearm. The right arm should be held so that the elbow rests against the rib cage with the rifle butt solidly against the shoulder.

Low Kneeling: In this position, the body should face slightly to the right of the target with the right leg bent so that the buttocks are placed squarely on the inside of the right foot which bears the weight of the body. The spine then bends forward with the left leg pointed almost directly at the target with the foot angled forward. This allows the left hand to be further forward on the stock and so the sling must be adjusted accordingly. Changes to position are made by rotating around the left foot.

Forward: Face the target. Angle the right leg away about 15 degrees and so that the right foot rests on the kneeling roll. The right buttock should rest on the right foot. The left leg should be pointed almost directly at the target (Figure 11-3). The lower left leg can be held vertically or angle forward, whichever is most comfortable. Most of the body's weight will be supported by the left leg and right knee. The arms are held in much the same way as for the high position but the sling will be shorter. The spine will bend forward but carry the head upright. Bone support is better in this position because it relies less on balance.

Fig 11-3. Forward kneeling position.

Sitting

Sitting is perhaps the easiest of all positions to master (Figure 11-4). Some shooters consider it to be steadier than the kneeling position. While sitting is the easiest position to assume, it does not provide the tripod like support of the kneeling or prone position.

Fig. 11-4. Sitting position.

To assume the sitting position, stand with hips and shoulders at right angle to the target with the rifle sling in place over the outside of the left wrist and high on the left upper arm. Cross your left leg over your right at the ankles and assume a sitting position. Rest your left elbow on your right knee and the right elbow on the right knee. The sling should pull tight enough to draw the left arm in slightly. Rest the butt securely against the right shoulder. Now lean forward slightly as you look through the rear sight. Sling tension should be sufficient to hold you at this position.

Prone

You will shoot best from the prone position; your center of gravity is a low as it can get, your body is in firm contact with a level surface which provides the largest area of support it is possible to achieve, and your arms and shoulder provide a tripod, steadied by the sling, on which to rest the rifle (Figure 11-5).

There are numerous variations of the prone position and you should use the one in which you are most comfortable. The basics of the prone position are as follows.

Adjust the sling before assuming the prone position, then lie down and see if the tension is correct. If not, move into a kneeling position and tighten or loosen the sling as needed, then lie down again. Do not attempt to adjust the sling while lying down as you will not achieve sufficient tension for good support. When you have the correct tension, mark your sling so that you can reset it quickly in the future.

Once in the prone position, your back muscles should be relaxed and your spine should be straight and about ten degrees to the right of the target. Your left leg should be in line with the spine with the left toe pointed in. The right leg should be bent outward at a 45 degree angle from the spine with the right toe pointing out. Adjust the position of the right leg until the right shoulder closes on the center of the position and the strain on the left elbow is lessened. This will also ease your breathing and reduce the beat of your pulse.

The left arm should be just to the left of the rifle, supporting it without strain. The left hand and wrist should be straight and the palm and fingers of the left hand should cradle the forend as it rests on the heel of the hand, not grasp it. Keep in mind that the left hand must be at least six inches above the ground according to International Shooting Union rules.

The one great of advantage on the prone position, beyond providing the steadiest shooting platform, is that the more comfortable you are, the better you will shoot.

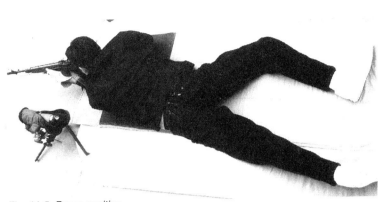
Fig. 11-5. Prone position.

Bench Rest

Bench resting is not a competitive shooting position for M14-type rifles, but it is a necessary position to master for sighting in and for testing different types and loads of ammunition. The bench should be about 33 inches high, give or take a few inches. More important is the height of the seat. A simple stool, preferably one that can be adjusted for height will serve. When seated, you should lean into the rifle naturally without having to contort your body unnaturally. The shooting bench should have a cutout into which your body can slide while still providing ample surface in front for the rifle and scope and to the right to support your right arm.

The rifle should be nested in a rifle rest or on sandbags. If a rifle rest is used, it should have a padded sandbag against which the forearm rests. Take your seat and place the rifle and sandbagged rest in front of you. Use a second sandbag under the toe of the stock. Adjust the position of the rifle so that the sights align with the target. Many shooters like to double their left fist and place it under the buttstock, ahead of the sandbag, to make minute adjustments. Snug the rifle against your shoulder and cheek, grasp the pistol grip of the stock so that the ball of the index finger rests on the trigger. Practice breath control and fire. Realign the rifle sights as before and fire again. Bench resting provides the steadiest of all shooting positions, short of a mechanical rest.

Fig. 11-6. Sling placement.

Slings

Needless to say, the rifle should always be fired with the sling. The military sling or a commercial variation thereof is most commonly used with the M14-type rifle in match shooting. The choice of a sling is a personal matter and involves finding one the shooter is comfortable wearing and can be adjusted easily.

The sling should be envisioned as the base of an inverted triangle. One side is the shooter's upper arm and the other is the shooter's forearm. Position the sling so that the forearm is not allowed to move forward. This transmits the rifle's weight to the back of the upper arm. If done correctly, the rifle is supported by bone and without effort from the arm's muscles.

Standing: The sling should pass over the back of the offhand wrist, around and above the elbow as high on the upper arm as is comfortable (Refer to Figure 11-1). The sling should be just tight enough to draw the arm inward slightly against the rib cage to provide bone-to-bone contact.

Kneeling/Sitting: The sling should be flat where it passes over the outside of the left wrist, and not twisted (refer to Figure 11-2). It should be buckled or worn high on the upper arm but should not be so tight that it cuts off circulation. If worn to low, it will lose its support value.

Prone: When assuming the prone position, the sling should already be in place. Kneel and place the rifle's butt on the shooting mat. Your offhand should be in position against the forward sling swivel (an excellent reason for wearing a shooting glove) with the sling passing over the outside of the wrist (remove wristwatches and bracelets first). The sling should be worn or buckled over the upper arm tight enough to keep it from sliding but not so tight as to cut off circulation (Figure 11-6). Do not allow the sling to pass over the middle of the arm or circulation will be cut off in the major artery that passes near the surface. At the very least it will pick up and transmit pulse beats.

Now lean forward using the rifle butt to steady yourself. Place the off hand on the mat and lean forward to assume a prone position. The sling should draw up to the proper tautness.

Sight Picture

Assuming that 1) your front and rear sights are in alignment because your rifle was assembled either by the factory or by an experienced gunsmith, 2) or you have sighted in the rifle properly as described in Table 11, 3) and you have entered adjustments for range and windage, you should look through the peep past the front sight post at the target. Make no attempt to center the front post in the peep — your eye will do so naturally — and do not try and focus on both the sight post and the target; focus on the target only.

Fig. 11-7. The proper sight picture.

The round black bull should sit exactly on top of your front sight post. Some shooters like to allow the merest sliver of slight between the top of the post and the bottom of the bull so that they know they have not raised the muzzle too high. When this image is attained, you have the proper sight picture. It only remains to hold it long enough to squeeze the trigger.

Some shooters make use of the wavering muzzle to allow the front sight post to pass across the bull. They squeeze the trigger at a predetermined moment as the post approaches the black center. A good theory but a bad practice as it makes consistency a matter of chance. Practice will teach you to hold the front sight steady on the bull.

Breathing

Breathing is easy to discuss, but difficult to accomplish. If done by the numbers, it becomes a habit. After taking the position, take one deep breath and puff it out. This oxygenates the lungs, builds up a slight reserve and clears out excess carbon dioxide which triggers the next breath reflex. Now take a second, normal breath and let half out. Achieve your sight picture and squeeze.

Heart and Pulse

If you are shooting in a match, adrenaline will be running and your breathing and heart rate will be up, both of which will inter-

Fig. 11-8. The well-equipped shooter.

fere with holding a consistent sight pattern. With practice, you can learn to control both. First, keep in mind that everybody else on the shooting line is also nervous and apprehensive. Secondly, do not fall for the ploys and distractions some shooters use to increase *your* nervousness. Concentrate on your own shooting, complete and study your score book between rounds. In other words, *focus*. Finally, while achieving your sight picture, control your breathing and listen and feel for your heart beat. With a little practice you will pick it up instantly. Trigger squeeze should occur between beats.

Miscellaneous Shooting Equipment

The match shooter, or one who is serious about shooting well, will need a spotting telescope and tripod or stand, shooting jacket, shooting glove, shooting box, shooting mat and shooting glasses (Figure 11-7). As there are so many fine variations of each available, we will only discuss them briefly. A spotting telescope of 20x, or one with a variable power range from 15-60x will serve well. Many prefer the variable power scopes as they can be adjusted for different ranges. Keep in mind that mirage, haze, dust, smog and other atmospheric conditions will often limit the scope's usefulness to between 20x and 40x power. Ideally, the scope should be mounted on tripod or other stand and placed beside the shooter so that he or she only has to turn his or her head to see through it, without disturbing the shooting position.

A comfortable shooting jacket, well made with adjustable buckles that permit adjusting the fit as well as padded elbows and shoulders will improve scores and make a big difference in comfort, especially in the prone position. A shooting glove is really a fingerless mitten for the offhand. It should have a non-slip coating or texture and be well padded around the edges. Leather is best.

Shooting glasses are mandatory. The lens should be safety glass and the necessary optical corrections can be incorporated into custom eye glasses. If like the author, you find your vision failing as you progress to and through middle age, consult an experienced optometrist or ophthalmologist, preferably one experienced with the special needs of shooters. The proper optical correction will do wonders for your scores. Consider also different colored lenses

56

to improve visibility: grey or green on bright days, amber on foggy or overcast days.

An excellent shooting mat is currently available from the Director of Civilian Marksmanship at a very good price. Another fine commercial mat is manufactured and sold by Dillon Precision Products, Inc. (See Appendix E). When purchasing a shooting mat, look for a reinforced bottom surface that will resist the cutting action of stones and twigs, sufficient padding to provide a cushion for hips, knees and elbows and a non-slip upper surface.

Finally, the shooting box. There are a number of boxes available on the market, ranging from the high- end Pachmyer down to well-made tool chests available at discount hardware stores. The author favors the latter for general rifle shooting. His is a top-opening box with three slide-out drawers. Into it, he has put an assortment of screwdrivers, small brass hammer, pliers, vise grips, steel and brass punches, cleaning cloth, cleaning solutions, lubricants, cleaning tips, patches, range finder, spare shooting glasses, heavy duty stapler and extra staples for tacking targets, black marking pen, steel ruler in decimal inches, pencil, notepad and scorebook. And a spare set of ear plugs. You will add other tools as time goes by. One of the most useful items in my shooting box is a small hand towel and bar of soap in a plastic box.

Always check match rules regarding the type and size of box you are allowed on the firing line. Obviously, my three drawer tool chest would be banned. For match use, it remains in the car while essentials are transferred to a folding shooting stool wearing a ballistic nylon hold-all. An excellent shooting stool (and other shooting accessories as well as fine match rifles) are available from Creedmore Sports, Inc. See Appendix E.

A rifle, ammunition, targets, a large bottle of drinking water or athletic drink such as Gatorade, a candy or granola bar and you are ready for a pleasant time at the range.

12: TROUBLE SHOOTING THE M14-TYPE RIFLE

When shooting the M14-type rifle, stoppages and failure to fire can happen for a variety of reasons. The Troubleshooting chart in Table 12 provides a list of most reasons why the rifle will fail to operate. For further explanation, consult the paragraphs following the table for detailed explanations of how to resolve the problem. If the problem is beyond your ability to resolve, consult an experienced gunsmith.

The following paragraphs provide detailed instructions for preventing the misfires outlined in the above chart. Years of experience in and out of the military by thousands of shooters have gone into the compilation of these explanations. If you fail to observe all precautions listed, you are doing so at the risk to your life and limbs, or worse, at the risk of another's. **BE SMART. BE CAREFUL!**

Note: *Read this paragraph carefully.* When a cartridge ignites inside the receiver of an M14-style rifle, it develops pressures in excess of 50,000 pounds per square inch. As long as the bolt is closed properly, this tremendous pressure will be channeled by the walls of the breech to drive the bullet down the bore. But if a "*hangfire*" should occur and you open the bolt to soon, *the cartridge will burst and shower you and anyone nearby with bits of metal cartridge case and very hot burning gases. You could be severely injured or possibly killed.* Learn the difference between a simple misfire and a hangfire.

Misfire, Hangfire, and Cookoff
Misfire
A misfire is a failure to fire. A misfire itself is not dangerous but since it cannot be immediately distinguished from a delay in the firing mechanism or from a hangfire it should always be considered as a hangfire for safety's sake.

A delay in functioning can result from the presence of foreign matter such as sand, grit, frost, ice, or oil and grease.

Hangfire
A hangfire is a delay caused by the failure of the powder charge to burn as quickly as it should. The amount of delay is unpredictable but, in most cases, will only be a few seconds at most. Thus, a hangfire cannot be distinguished immediately from a misfire, so do not assume that a failure of the weapon to fire is a *misfire*; in fact, it may prove to be a *hangfire*.

WARNING: When a misfire/hangfire occurs, keep the rifle's muzzle *pointed down range* until the problem is resolved.

Cookoff
A cookoff occurs when a cartridge is chambered in the rifle's breech which has become so hot that it explodes the primer in the case and ignites the propelling charge. To prevent a cookoff, a round should never be loaded into a hot weapon unless it is to be fired within 5 to 10 seconds maximum.

Warning: A live round should never be left in a hot weapon any longer than circumstances require because of the possibility of a cookoff.

Procedures for Removing a Round in Case of Failure to Fire
After failure to fire. The following precautions should be observed in case of a failure to fire for any reason.
1. Keep the weapon trained on the target downrange and see that all personnel remain clear of the muzzle.
2. Before retracting the bolt and removing the round, make certain that no one is near you.
3. Make certain the round, after removal from the weapon, is kept separate from other rounds until it has been determined whether the round or the firing mechanism was at fault. If the weapon is found to be at fault, the round may be reloaded and fired after correcting the cause of the failure to fire. If the cartridge is defective, crush the case or twist the bullet to one side with a pair of pliers so that it cannot be reused, then discard safely.

Time Interval. Following a failure to fire, the U.S. Army has prescribed the following time intervals:
1. Do not open the bolt for at least *5 seconds* to insure against an explosion outside of the gun in event a hangfire develops.
2. If the barrel is hot, and a misfire stops operation of the gun, wait *5 seconds* with the round locked in the chamber to insure against hangfire dangers (a hangfire will occur within *5 seconds* after the primer is struck), then extract the round immediately to prevent cookoff.
3. If the round cannot be extracted within an additional *5 seconds*, it must remain locked in the chamber with the muzzle pointed in a safe direction for at least *5 minutes* due to the possibility of a cookoff.

One hundred and fifty rounds fired within a 2-minute interval will heat a barrel enough to produce a cookoff.

Table 12
Troubleshooting Chart

Malfunction	Probable Cause	Corrective Action
Failure to load	Dirty or deformed ammunition	Clean ammunition or replace
	Dented magazine or bent or deformed magazine lips	Replace magazine
	Broken magazine spring	Replace spring
	Broken or damaged floor plate	Replace floor plate
Magazine inserts with difficulty	You are inserting it improperly	Insert front of magazine deep into well and press against front, then rock the back end up and into place until it latches
	Broken or deformed magazine	Replace magazine
	Round not seated properly —bullet protruding	Remove and reinsert
	Excessive dirt in receiver well	Clean
	Deformed or damaged operating rod spring guide	Replace
	Magazine latch jammed	Clean or replace
Magazine will not remain in rifle	Magazine latch or latch spring damaged or deformed	Replace
	Magazine latch plate damaged or missing	Replace magazine
	Deformed or damaged operating rod spring guide	Replace
	Locking recess at top front of magazine deformed	Consult a gunsmith
	Magazine did not latch securely	Try again
Failure to feed	Weak or broken magazine spring	Replace
	Damaged or deformed magazine	Replace
	Damaged or deformed stripping lug on bolt	Consult a gunsmith for head space check, replace

	Dirty ammunition and/or magazine	Clean or replace
	Weak or broken operating rod spring	Replace
	Damaged operating rod or otherwise restricted motion	Replace
Bolt fails to close properly	Cartridge case holding bolt out of battery	Pull bolt to rear and remove
	Dirty chamber	Clean chamber
	Extractor did not snap over cartridge case rim	Clean bolt assembly and extractor recess in breech face of barrel. Replace worn extractor and/or spring and plunger
	Frozen or blocked ejector spring and plunger	Replace ejector parts
	Restricted movement of, or damaged operating rod	Replace
	Bolt not fully locked into receiver	Remove any foreign substances restricting bolt movement. If bolt still refuses to lock, consult a gunsmith
	Weak or broken operating rod spring	Replace
	Damaged receiver	Consult a gunsmith. Do not attempt to fire rifle again
Rifle Fails to Fire	Bolt not fully forward and locked	See above
	Defective ammunition	Follow misfire procedure.
	Firing pin worn or damaged,	Examine firing pin for breaks, burrs or foreign matter. Clean bolt and firing pin tunnel. Replace if necessary
	Broken hammer	Replace
	Weak or broken hammer spring	Replace
	Hammer lugs, trigger lugs or sear worn or broken, causing hammer to ride the bolt forward	Replace worn or broken part
Short Recoil—new cartridge does not load	Gas plug loose or missing	Tighten or replace
	Operating rod movement restricted	Inspect for reason. Check for obstructions or broken or worn operating rod spring

	Bolt is binding	Clean receiver, lubricate properly. Check for obstructions in the bolt track or extractor recess
	Gas cylinder lock not fully installed so that gas port is blocked	Reinstall properly
	Gas piston movement restricted	Clean gas cylinder and piston. If damaged, replace
	Damaged connector assembly	Consult a gunsmith
	Partially closed gas (spindle) valve	Turn valve to vertical position at right angle to bore
	Improper lubrication in cold weather	Clean and lubricate properly
	Defective ammunition	Replace ammunition
Failure to Extract	Gas (spindle) valve closed	Turn valve to vertical position
	Cartridge stuck in chamber	Use cleaning rod or broken shell extractor to remove cartridge case. Clean remaining ammunition
	Short recoil	See Short Recoil Section above
	Damaged or deformed extractor	Replace extractor
	Weak, deformed, broken or frozen extractor plunger assembly	Replace extractor assembly
	Ruptured or separated cartridge, head sheared off	Use broken shell extractor to remove
Failure to Eject	Short recoil	See Short Recoil Section
	Weak, deformed, broken or frozen ejector spring and plunger	Replace ejector spring and plunger assembly
Failure to Hold Bolt Rearward	Damaged or deformed magazine follower	Replace magazine or follower
	Damaged or deformed bolt lock	Consult a gunsmith
	Bolt lock movement restricted	Clean bolt lock recess in receiver. If condition persists, consult a gunsmith
	Weak or broken magazine spring	Replace magazine or magazine spring

Operation Under Unusual Conditions

Special care in cleaning and lubrication must be observed where extremes of temperature, humidity, and atmospheric conditions are present or anticipated. Proper cleaning, lubrication, storage, and handling of lubricants not only insure operation and functioning but also guard against excessive wear of the working parts and deterioration of the materiel.

Cold Climate Operation. In climates where the temperature is consistently below 0°F, special precautions are required. Generally, extreme cold will cause lubricants to congeal. Therefore, the weapon and bipod should be thoroughly cleaned of all lubricants or grease with rifle bore cleaner and be re-lubricated with a low-temperature lubricant. When in very cold conditions, move the various controls through their entire range at frequent intervals to keep them from freezing in place and to reduce the effort required to operate them. When the rifle must be carried or stored outside for short intervals, pay particular attention to protecting it with a cover fastened so that snow, ice, or moisture will be kept out of the operating parts. Provide as much protection as possible for all parts of the materiel.

Hot Climate Operation

When operating in hot climates, the film of oil necessary for operation and preservation will dissipate quickly. Inspect the rifle frequently, paying particular attention to all hidden surfaces such as bolt and roller, operating rod and recess, cam surface and bolt locking recess in receiver, and the yoke assembly and leg assemblies of the bipod where corrosion might occur and not be noticed. Perspiration from the hands is a contributing factor to rusting because it contains acids and salts. After handling, clean, wipe dry, and restore the oil film using a good gun oil or military lubricant for small arms. Use a patch wetted with gun oil.

Hot, Dry Climates

When operating in hot, dry climates, clean and oil the bore of the rifle more frequently than usual.

Hot, Damp, and Salty Atmosphere

Inspect the rifle and bipod frequently when operating in hot, moist areas. Clean and lubricate the bore and exposed metal surfaces more frequently than prescribed for normal service. Moist and salty atmospheres have a tendency to emulsify oils and greases and destroy their rust preventive qualities. Inspect all parts frequently for corrosion. When the rifle and bipod are not in use, cover surfaces with a good grade of rifle lubricating oil.

Operation Under Sandy or Muddy Conditions

When in sandy areas, clean and lubricate the rifle and bipod more frequently. Exercise particular care to keep sand out of the mechanism when inspecting and lubricating the rifle. Shield parts from flying sand during disassembly and assembly. Before firing in sandy areas, remove the lubricant from bolt, barrel and receiver, connector assembly, operating rod, firing mechanism, and bipod, as they will pick up sand and form an abrasive which will cause rapid wear. There is *less wear* on dry surfaces than when coated with lubricant contaminated with sand. Clean and lubricate all exposed parts after firing.

Mud

Clean and lubricate the rifle and bipod as soon as possible when operating in muddy areas. Exercise particular care and make certain all mud is removed and that the mechanism is thoroughly dry before lubricating. Clean and lubricate all exposed parts when the shooting session is over.

Lubrication

First clean metal parts with solvent and dry thoroughly. Apply a light coat of rifle grease lubriplate 130A or other suitable lubricating grease to the following surfaces: 1) Bolt locking lugs, operating lug, and recesses. 2) Bolt guide. 3) Antifriction roller on bolt. 4) Operating rod guide groove on side of the receiver.

Lubrication Under Unusual Conditions

Depending on where the rifle is being used, you should reduce or increase lubrication as outlined above to compensate for abnormal operation and extreme conditions.

Extreme Cold-Weather Lubrication.

Apply a light coat of low temperature lubricating oil to the rifle and bipod and exercise weapon frequently when the temperature is below O° F.

Extreme Hot-Weather Lubrication

Special lubricants will ordinarily not be required at extremely high temperatures, as lubricants prescribed for temperatures above O° F, provide adequate protection.

Lubrication for Humid and Wet Air Conditions. High humidity, moisture, or salt air contaminate lubricants, necessitating more frequent service.

Before-Immersion Lubrication

No special lubrication is required if the rifle will be used in extremely wet areas or in heavy rain.

After-Immersion Lubrication

After immersion, disassemble the rifle as far as practical and thoroughly dry all parts. If the rifle was immersed in salt water, soak the parts in fresh water for several minutes and rinse and dry thoroughly. Coat each part with lubricating oil, paying special attention to slots, screw holes and other hard to reach places. Reassemble the rifle and check carefully in succeeding days to spot any rust that develops.

Lubrication After Operation Under Sandy or Dusty Conditions

Under dusty or sandy conditions, clean and inspect all lubricated surfaces for fouled lubricants. Clean thoroughly and re-lubricate.

Preventive Maintenance for Civilian Shooters

It is not necessary for civilian shooters to inspect the rifle according to a set schedule as their rifles do not receive the same rate of use as military rifles. Instead, inspect the rifle and its component parts before and after use. Before storing for long periods, lubricate all metal parts, including the bore. You may even want to apply a light coat of furniture or auto wax to the wooden stock to seal in oils. Inspect at frequent intervals, depending on how humid your climate is. Also inspect for signs of rust or corrosion at least monthly; more often during rainy weather or in the winter. Keep in mind that the cycle of cold night-warm daytime temperatures in your home or other storage facility can cause moisture to form on metal parts.

During use, watch for signs of wear or breakage. Repair or replace any parts that show signs of wear before they cause problems.

Cleaning Instructions

Civilian shooters need not follow the approved military procedure for cleaning their M14-type rifles as they will not ordinarily be shooting under extreme conditions nor in as heavy a volume. The following military cleaning instructions are given here for historical interest. They are followed by less-rigorous cleaning procedures that will suit civilian shooters just as well and cause less wear.

The M14 cleaning kit (Figure 12-1) consisted of 1) bore brush, 2) chamber brush, 3) cloth case, 4) plastic tube for lubricant, 5) loop for holding patch, 6) rod sections (3), 7) combination tool.
The cleaning kit, lubricant tube and combination tool were was stored in the buttstock. The kit was designed as a field expedient; serious shooters should substitute a one-piece nylon-coated or brass rod and a brass or aluminum loop to prevent wear in the bore or at the ends of the lands and grooves at the muzzle.

Military Cleaning Instructions

Immediately after firing, thoroughly clean the bore with a brass wire bore brush saturated with rifle bore cleaner. Make certain that all surfaces including the rifling are well soaked.

After cleaning with the bore brush, the bore should be swabbed with flannel cleaning patches making certain no trace of burned powder, or other foreign substances are left. It may be necessary to reapply bore cleaner to one or more patches. Finish with a dry patch.

Apply a light coat of gun oil to the bore by soaking a patch and running it back and forth through the bore several times.

The chamber should be cleaned with a cleaning brush as follows:
When the rifle is assembled. Screw the threaded end of cleaning rod section into ratchet base of brush. Remove the magazine. Apply a light coat of rifle bore cleaner to the chamber. Draw the bolt rearward to engage the bolt lock, holding the stock to keep the rifle from flipping over and damaging the handguard.

Insert the brush in the chamber with thumb pushing against the base. Pull the operating rod to the rear, release the bolt lock and ease operating rod and bolt all the way forward, seating the brush in chamber. Move rod section from side-to-side several times.

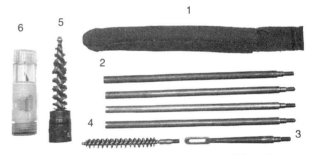

Fig. 12-1. The M14 military cleaning kit: 1) Case, 2) four-piece cleaning rod, 3) patch holder or loop, 4) bore brush, 5) chamber brush and 6) lubricant bottle.

Grasp the cleaning rod section as close to the receiver as possible, with the fingers pulling rearward and thumb exerting a forward pressure on the end of the rod. Pull rearward until the brush clears the chamber. Grasp the operating rod handle, relieving tension on the brush, and remove the brush from the

Fig. 12-2. M14 combination tool. The cylinder depending from the left side is the attaching point for the cleaning rod.

receiver. Apply a light coat of gun oil to the chamber, and close the bolt.
When the rifle is disassembled. Insert the brush in chamber with your thumb exerting pressure on the base of brush. Move the rod section from side-to-side several times. Remove the brush from the chamber and apply a light coat of bore lubricating oil.

To clean the gas spindle valve, push in and rotate the valve with a tool several times until the carbon breaks loose. *Do not attempt to disassemble the valve.* If the valve is stuck, use a block of wood or a plastic hammer (not a steel hammer) to drive the valve from side to side, until valve loosens and can be rotated easily.

Use rifle bore cleaner to clean all parts which have been exposed to powder fouling: gas cylinder, piston, and plug. Keep in mind that rifle bore cleaner is not a lubricant and should not be used as such.

Rifle bore cleaner can also be used to loosen and remove carbon from the gas cylinder, piston and plug. These components are made from corrosion-resistant steel which discolors as a result of firing. This is a normal condition.

Note: Using abrasives to shine these components will the cause the rifle to malfunction. Also, do not lubricate these components. They are to be cleaned only with mineral spirits (paint thinner) to wash away oil and grease.

Note: Do not use metal tools to scrape carbon deposits from these parts. Hard carbon residues can be cleaned with special solvents made for this purpose.

Civilian Shooter's Cleaning Instructions

When shooting commercial or American military ammunition made after the mid-1950s, it is not necessary to scrub the bore with a metal brush after every use. Every second or third time will prove satisfactory. After every use, soak a cloth patch in bore solvent and using a bore guide, clean the bore by running the cleaning rod from muzzle to breech ten times. Follow with dry patches until all traces of fouling are removed. After an especially heavy shooting session, it may be necessary to use a solvent-soaked patch, two or even three times.

When using a bore brush, always use either a brass or nylon brush, *never a stainless steel brush*. Always use a bore guide to prevent the cleaning rod from wearing against the lands. If possible, use a commercial, full length, rubber or nylon coated cleaning rod rather than the jointed military rods which flex excessively and can wear against the lands.

For the finest accuracy, it is important to remove cooper fouling from the rifling. Use a good grade of copper fouling remover after every third or fourth shooting session, or when accuracy appears to be degrading. Follow the instructions on the container.

To clean the chamber, follow the instructions given above in the Military Cleaning section, but use the wire brush gently and swab out with cloth patches.

All other instructions from Military Cleaning apply.

Cleaning the Stock Assembly

When cleaning the wooden or plastic surfaces of the stock assembly, remove dirt, grease and carbon, by wiping with dry cloth. If the stock is extremely dirty, use a mild solution of liquid dishwashing detergent applied with a sponge. If the wooden stock is especially dirty, lemon oil applied to a soft cloth will usually remove the dirt or grease without damaging the finish. Plastic (fiberglass) stocks can be further cleaned by wiping with alcohol. Apply linseed oil sparingly to wood stocks and rub in well to prohibit absorption of moisture.

Note: Do not apply linseed oil to areas next to the barrel. Heat from the barrel will cause it to smoulder, obscuring the shooter's vision. Wipe linseed oil from all metal parts before it dries.

Care of Sling, Envelopes, Scabbards, and Stock Assembly

To prevent mildew, shake out and air web straps and canvas items for several hours at frequent intervals. Mildewed canvas can be cleaned by scrubbing with a dry brush. Do not use water until all traces of mildew have been brushed away. Examine the area carefully for rotting or weakening by stretching and pulling it. If fabric shows indication of loss of tensile strength, it is probably not worth retreatment. Oil and grease may be removed by scrubbing with soap and water. Rinse well with water and dry.

Never use gasoline or other organic solvents to remove oil or grease from canvas. Use a good laundry detergent, rinse and dry thoroughly before folding.

THE DEVELOPMENT AND SERVICE LIFE OF THE M14 RIFLE

Genesis

In the summer of 1945, Ordnance Engineers at the Springfield National Armory had completed development of a new rifle designated the T20E2 (the T stood for test). It looked like a G.I. M1 Garand except for a funny looking attachment on the muzzle called a recoil check, and a 20 round magazine. And a small switch above the trigger. The T20E2 was a selective fire version of the M1 Garand, the rifle that General George Patton had called "the greatest battle implement ever developed" (Figure A-1).

For several years, development engineers at Springfield, under the direction of Colonel René R. Studler, Chief of Small Arms Research Development, had been working on improvements to the M1 Garand, and on a selective fire version of the rifle. By the late summer of 1945, tests had shown that the new rifle was ready for service. The T20E2 was not as reliable as the M1 Garand in the parts breakage department and the recoil of the powerful .30-06 cartridge fired on full automatic was exhausting. But if the rifle had been introduced in the last months of World War II, it would have been received by combat troops with glee. Only the end of that war in August 1945 prevented the T20E2 from being placed in production.

Colonel Studler also headed another project at Springfield, the development of a smaller .30 caliber cartridge that while reducing recoil, would maintain the same ballistics as the venerable .30-06. It sounded like an impossible task but

Fig. A-1. Infantrymen of the 4th Armored Division fire at German troops during the advance to relieve Bastonge 27 December 1944. US Army Photo

Colonel Studler was convinced it could be done. Improvements in smokeless gunpowder realized earlier in the war coupled with information from the German development of the medium caliber *sturmgeweher* cartridge, plus a large helping of engineering skill from Winchester, resulted in the .308 cartridge which was a third smaller and lighter than the .30-06 but which had virtually the same ballistics to a range of 600 yards. The new cartridge was designated the T65. Later, it would be adopted by the U.S. Army, and by NATO, as the 7.62 x 51 mm NATO cartridge.

In the meantime, work had continued on a number of fronts. Several new lightweight rifle designs were developed and tested using the T65 cartridge. John C. Garand, the inventor and developer of both the M1 Garand and the T20E2 continued to develop the selective fire T20 concept. By 1950, it had evolved into a heavy barreled rifle with a new recoil reducer. In tests against the Model 1919 Browning Automatic Rifle, the T20E2 was pronounced superior in many respects, but not all. Soldiers assigned to shoot the rifle noted that under automatic fire the stock had a tendency to hammer the cheek and the buttplate slipped from the shoulder.

By August 22, 1952 and the start of a new series of trials, the situation had become truly complicated. Two American rifle designs, the T44 (using a modification of the Garand gas system) and the T47 (using a falling bolt mechanism), were being tested against the Belgian *Fusil Leger Automatique* (FAL) and the British EM-2 design. When the tests were completed on December 29, 1952, the FAL (Figure A-2) had proved to be the best of the designs. The British EM-2 and the American T47 were dropped from consideration. Orders were given

Fig. A-2. Adopted by over 90 nations, the **Fusil Leger Automatique** became the Free World's battle rifle during the early and mid-years of the Cold War.

to continue the development of both the FAL (designated the T48) and the T44.

The T44 was pushed hard by the Ordnance Corps. The report made by the AFF No. 3 Trials Board on April 20, 1952 found the rifle to be as accurate, effective, safe and easy to use as the M1 Garand. The T44 was less accurate in automatic fire than the M1 Garand in semiautomatic fire—which was expected. But the T44 was found to be more durable and reliable and it weighed 1.52 pounds less.

The final series of tests were scheduled for 1956 and were to include a series of shoot-outs between the T44 and the T48 FAL. Glitches and delays reduced the scope of the tests but when the smoke cleared and the reports were all written, the T44 had become the clear choice.

On May 1, 1957, Secretary of the Army, Wilbur H. Bruckner announced that the T44 had been redesignated the M14 and adopted as the standard rifle of the U.S. Army.

Production Begins

The first production order was given to Springfield Armory on March 26, 1958 for 15,600 rifles. The first production rifle was serial numbered 2000 (previous numbers had been used up by development and testing). But because of startup production problems, the first rifles were not delivered until July 1959. In all, Springfield received four production orders for a total of 167,173 rifles, of which 167,107 were actually delivered.

Because of other commitments, Springfield did not have the capacity to produce the M14 in sufficient quantity to equip the U.S. military. The Ordnance Department, returning to a practice followed previously, let contracts to commercial manufacturers as it had during WW II and the Korean War.

Harrington & Richardson received five separate orders between 1959 and 1963 for a total of 537,512 rifles. They actually delivered 113 more than called for, making them the largest supplier of M14 rifles.

Winchester received their first order in 1959, a second in 1960 and the third and fourth in 1962 and 1963 for a total of 356,510 rifles. And they delivered that exact number.

Thompson-Ramo-Wooldridge (TRW) was an aerospace concern but they also had strong expertise in precision manufacturing techniques. They were awarded contracts in 1961 and again in 1963 for a total of 319,163 rifles. And they delivered 314,789.

Table A1 provides the serial number ranges assigned by the Ordnance Department to the four manufacturers. The total number of M14s reported delivered by the manufacturers were recorded at 1,376,031. This number is at odds with government records which indicated acceptance of 1,380,358 M14 rifles, a discrepancy of 4,327 M14s.

Table A1
M14 Serial Number Ranges

Serial No. Range	Manufacture
2,000 - 9,213	Springfield National Armory
9,214 - 54,213	Winchester Repeating Firearms
54,214 - 89,213	Harrington & Richardson
89,214 - 121,950	Springfield National Armory
121,951 -205,613	Winchester Repeating Firearms
205,614 - 280,713	Harrington & Richardson
280,714 - 289,213	Apparently not assigned
289,214 - 292,514	Harrington & Richardson
292,215 - 333,764	Springfield National Armory
333,765 - 352,678	Harrington & Richardson
352,679 - 363,471	Springfield National Armory
363,472 - 516,471	Harrington & Richardson
516,472 - 565,496	Springfield Armory
565,497 - 577,896	Winchester Repeating Firearms
577,897 - 578,500	Springfield National Armory
578,501 - 688,500	Thompson, Ramo, Wooldridge
688,501 - 1,031,000	Harrington & Richardson
1,031,001 -1,292,001	Winchester Repeating Firearms
1,292,002 - 1,512,164	Thompson, Ramo, Wooldridge
1,512,165 - 1,600,164	Springfield National Armory
1,600,165 - 1,601,400	Thompson, Ramo, Wooldridge

Service Use

The M14 replaced the M1 Garand slowly during the first two years. In fact, the M1 Garand was still in service with many National Guard units when the M14 was withdrawn in 1966.

The M14 was manufactured at four factories: 1) The Springfield National Armory, 2) Harrington & Richardson Arms, 3) Winchester (New Haven) and 4) by Thompson Ramo Wooldridge (TRW). Each manufacturer has its partisans but after each company's teething troubles were solved, there really was very little difference between them in terms of reliability and safety.

To the end of its days, the M1 Garand experienced mild problems. The M14's design seemed to have cured most of these. The basic action—expanded gas tapped from the barrel and bled through a port to strike a piston/operating rod which caused it to move backward, drawing the bolt with it—remained the same. But the M1's bulky gas cylinder hanging on the end of the barrel was reduced in size and moved eight inches behind the muzzle. The relocated gas valve allowed the M14 to provide better accuracy as the motion of the shorter operating rod and bolt was less abrupt and had a smaller effect on the orientation of the bore's axis during cycling.

John C. Garand also modified the way the gas was used to operate the action in the M14. When a cartridge was fired, some of the hot expanding gases that drove the bullet up the barrel were bled away through a port in the barrel, just as in the M1. But in the M14, the gases expanded into a hollow gas piston rather than impacting against a solid piston head as in the M1. When the piston was filled, it began to move to the rear, pulling the gas vent out of alignment with the gas port and shutting of the further flow of gas. The piston traveled 1.5 inches to the rear where it uncovered another vent which released the gases trapped in the hollow piston. The milder action reduced but did not eliminate the parts breakage problems.

In the M14, the gas flow could be shut off to launch grenades by turning an adjustable gas valve. If the soldier did not intend to launch more grenades, he turned the gas valve back on and the rifle resumed its semiautomatic or automatic function.

In the M14, the M1's eight round en block clip had given way to a twenty round magazine. This meant that the soldier could "top up his magazine" at any time, which he could not do with the M1's en block clip. And when the ammunition was exhausted, the clip did not bounce out of the breech with a distinctive ping to alert the enemy to the fact that your weapon was empty.

The M14 was a selective fire weapon; that is, it could be fired in the semiautomatic mode — one round per trigger squeeze — or on full automatic — multiple rounds per trigger squeeze. However, it was quickly discovered under field conditions that the full automatic mode in the M14 was next to useless for anything but forcing the enemy to keep their heads down. The 7.62 x 51 mm NATO cartridge produced more recoil than most soldiers could handle during full auto fire. Accordingly, the full automatic mode on the majority of M14s issued for service was disabled.

But the M14 in full automatic still had a role to play. In every rifle squad, at least two M14s were equipped with a bipod and retained their full auto capability. These rifles served as squad automatics, fulfilling the role once taken by the M1919 Browning Automatic Rifle. But even that limited task was soon superseded by the M60 machine gun.

Full Auto Fire

The fire selector switch was located on the right side of the receiver, near the rear. The switch engaged the connector, a rectangular lever with an eccentric cam that moved the sear release backward into contact with the sear and pulled the connector assembly back into contact with the operating rod.

As the bolt drove the hammer to rear, a lip on the sear was positioned to engage the hooks on the hammer and hold it in the cocked position. As the bolt moved forward and locked, a projection on the operating rod engaged the hook on the connector and pulled it forward. That caused the sear release to rotate, pushing the sear rearward and releasing the hammer to be driven forward by its spring to fire the cartridge. Unless the trigger was released, the cycle occurred again.

Rearming With the M14

Even though the M14 was standardized in early 1957, not a single production rifle was produced until July 1959. Congress had dictated that commercial firearms manufactur-

Fig. A-3. A solider armed with an M14 watches the destruction of a Viet Cong tunnel complex. US Army Photo

ers were to be involved in the production of the M14, as they had so successfully been in the production of the M1 Garand both during and after World War II. But the problems involved in getting Congress to appropriate sufficient funds and then bringing three additional manufacturers on line successfully took more than two years to solve.

Vietnam and Power Politics

The M14 received its baptism of fire in Vietnam as early as 1961 (Figure A-3). U.S. Army advisers to the military forces of the Republic of Vietnam used the M14 extensively in combat with the Viet Cong (Figure A-4). But the rifle was too large and heavy for the slightly built Vietnamese soldiers to use effectively and so its distribution was largely limited to Americans (Figure A-5). Even this limited combat showed up new problems. In spite of changes in the gas system to reduce impact, parts breakage hovered around the unacceptable point.

At the same time, questions arose regarding the rifle's accuracy. Many rumors were floating about, some dealing with he various manufacturer's ability to build accurate rifles, others with the ammunition. As it turned out a combination of factors were involved and all were solved fairly easily.

Fig. A-4. M14-equipped 3rd Division Marines were the first U.S. combat troops to arrive in Vietnam on 8 March 1965. USMC photo

During this period, the Army was also investigating Eugene Stoner's new AR15 rifle, but the Byzantine power politics of the Ordnance Department were stalling its development. Proponents of the M14, having taken years to get the rifle accepted, were now so firmly entrenched that they were in a position to prevent further development of the AR15 concept.

Secretary of Defense Robert McNamara finally demanded a full investigation not only of past M14 vs. the M16 tests

Fig. A-5. A Marine of Company C, 2nd Battalion, 1st Marines on patrol in Vietnam. USMC photo

but of the M14's performance in combat. The Army's Inspector General did indeed find that several tests had been rigged to show the AR15 in a poor light. In fact, the AR15 — soon to be the M16 — had outperformed the M14 in almost every category. That, and the breakage problem made up the Pentagon's collective minds.

Secretary McNamara announced on January 23, 1963 that when that year's production contracts for the M14 were filled, all further procurement of the rifle would be terminated. At the same time, he announced what was expected to be a one time buy of 85,000 AR15 rifles for the Army and 19,000 for the Air Force (Figure A-6).

The M15

By the late 1950s, the standard squad automatic weapon, the M1918A1 Browning Automatic Rifle (BAR) was forty years old. Developed in the closing stages of World War I, the BAR

in its three major configurations had served well and faithfully through World War II, the Korean War and a host of smaller, conflicts. But at 19.4 pounds and chambered for the now obsolete .30-06 cartridge, the BAR was too heavy and cumbersome for the modern battlefield.

Engineers at the Ordnance Department decided to see if the M14 could be developed into a squad automatic rifle. Doing so would save millions in the development costs of a new weapon and simplify logistics requirements. A weapons development project designated T44E5 was begun. Because a squad automatic weapon would fire many times more than an infantry rifle, a reinforced, heavy weight, chrome-lined barrel was developed. A detachable bipod was also designed to allow the weapon to be fired from the prone position. Subsequent testing showed the need for a hinged buttplate similar to that already developed for the M1918A1. It was hoped that the hinged buttplate would make the weapon more controllable in full automatic fire.

Unfortunately, further testing showed that even with the bipod and the hinged buttplate, the M15 was inaccurate because of excessive muzzle climb and recoil. The M15 program was canceled late in 1959.

The M14A1

But the Army still needed a squad automatic weapon to replace the BAR. The Ordnance Department concentrated on improved controllability during full auto fire. An exaggerated pistol grip stock (Figure A-7) and muzzle stabilizer were designed (Figure A-8). The heavy barrel was dispensed with but the M2 Bipod was retained. As the M14E2, the new rifle was tested thoroughly from 1963 to 1967 when it was finally adopted as the M14A1. But further M14 production had already been canceled and the Army decided that the M60 Machine Gun could provide far better full auto support than M14A1. Today, the only legacy of the M14A1 that remains are pistol-gripped M14 stocks available at gun shows and from suppliers manufactured under contract by Canadian Arsenals, Ltd.

Fig. A-7. M14A1 Pistol Grip Stock.

The Service Life of the M14 Ends

The M14 would remain the "Standard A" rifle until January 1, 1968, but the M16, accepted in 1964, was fast displacing it in Southeast Asia. When M14 procurement was canceled, the

Fleet Marine Force had only been completely equipped with the M14 for three months. And the Army had not even managed to completely reequip itself with the new rifle. Hundreds of thousands of M1 Garands were still in service, particularly in Reserve and National Guard units. Interestingly enough, the M14 was originally characterized as an inherently inaccurate rifle by virtually every unbiased review board which had tested it. Experienced military armorers pointed out that it was impossible to develop an accurate rifle unless 1) the receiver was solidly bedded in the stock, 2) the barrel was free-floated—did not touch any other part of the rifle at any time, 3) the barrel was specifically tuned for accurate shooting.

Fig. A-8. This muzzle brake was designed for installation on the M14A1. The clamp below the muzzle brake fastened to the bayonet mount.

The M14 Soldiers On

The U.S. service rifle is always used in the National Matches which are Department of Defense-sponsored shooting contests that blend military and civilian participants (Figure A-9). Historically, the matches—which have been held since the first decade of the 20th Century—have contributed a great deal to the development not only of expert marksmen for military service, but the development of excellent weapons as well.

The program to develop a National Match M14 rifle to replace the M1 National Match rifle began in 1959 and the first rifles were built in 1962. New production rifles were used from 1962 to 1964; after because production had ceased, existing M14 rifles were rebuilt into National Match rifles.

Briefly, the M14 National match rifle differed from the standard issue service rifle in the following particulars:

1) The bore was held to half the tolerance as the service rifle and was not chrome plated.

2) The receiver was fiberglass-bedded in the stock.

3) Certain of the rifle's parts were hand-fitted and assembled.

4) An improved rear sight allowed elevation and windage adjustments in 1/2 minute of angle increments.

5) The selector shaft, sear release, selector lock and receiver sear were welded so that the rifle would fire in the semiautomatic mode only.

A more detailed description of the M14 as the National Match rifle is given in Chapter 3.

The M21—Snipers in Vietnam

The need for an effective sniper rifle became apparent during the War in Vietnam. During the early years, ancient M1Cs, M1Ds and MC52s — and even a few Model 1903A4s — were issued to troops in the field. But they proved to be marginal performers at best.

The Viet Cong and the North Vietnamese regulars were using Russian-made Mosin-Nagant and Dragunov SVD sniper rifles, and they showed how effective well-trained snipers could be. In response, both the Army and the Marines Corps established sniper training schools and worked hard to develop suitable rifles. The Winchester Model 70, with a variety of telescopic sights, was tested as was the Remington Model 700 BDL which, in a much modified version built by USMC armorers, was soon adopted by the Marine Corps as the M40 Sniper Rifle. But the Army discovered that the National Match M14 fitted with a range finding telescopic sight served admirably as a sniper weapon.

Fig. A-9. Brigadier General Harry J Mott, then Deputy Chief, Army Reserve, fires an M14 National Match Rifle for score.

After long experimentation and field testing it was finally standardized as the M21 Sniper Rifle. By 1970, U.S. Army and Marine Corps snipers were actively engaged in the field and both services compiled impressive records. The M21 continued to as the designated sniper rifle of the U.S. Army until the M24 Sniper Weapons System was adopted in 1988. But it still continues to serve the Army as an auxiliary sniper weapon. Both the M21 and the M24 saw extensive service during the Persian Gulf War.

See Chapter 4 for a more detailed discussion.

NATIONAL MATCH RIFLES
DEVELOPED BY THE U.S. ARMY MARKSMANSHIP TRAINING UNIT

1967 National Match Rifle, U.S. Cal. 7.62 mm, M14

1. All components shall conform to the latest design.
2. All wooden components shall be of solid heartwood with the direction of grain parallel to the longitudinal axis of stock.
3. The stock shall be glass bedded and custom fitted to barrel and receiver assembly and trigger housing assembly. The stock assembly and the trigger housing assembly shall be identified with last four digits of the receiver serial number. These assemblies shall not be interchanged after glass bedding process has been completed. Stock liners are bedded with the stocks. The rear legs of the receiver shall have an equal bearing on the recoil shoulders of the stock liner.
4. The stock shall be free from contact with the barrel.
5. Stock ferrule shall not contact lower portion of front band longitudinally. There shall be 1/64" minimum clearance. Vertically, the stock ferrule shall contact the front band.
6. The stock shall have a clearance in the area between rear of receiver bedding surface and receiver rail bedding surfaces.
7. Clamping of the trigger guard shall have a definite resistance at a distance of 1/4 to 3/8 inches from the full lock position.
8. Gas cylinder shall fit tightly on the barrel diameter and the splines. There shall be no power rotational movement of the gas cylinder.
9. Gas cylinder shall be brought forward against the lock before tightening the gas cylinder plug.
10. The gas cylinder plug shall be tightened to 15 ft. lbs +/- 2 pounds torque.
11. In assembly, the gas cylinder lock shall be hand tightened against the shoulder on the barrel within a range of slightly beyond the 6 o'clock position but not in excess of 210 degrees (1 o'clock) past the 6 o'clock position. The gas cylinder lock shall then be "backed off" the minimum distance necessary to align with the gas cylinder at the 6 o'clock position.
12. Bore diameter shall be 0.300 +/- .001. Groove diameter shall be 0.3075 +/- .001. Any taper of the bore shall be within dimensional limits and be diminishing from breech to muzzle. The barrel muzzle shall be crowned concentric with bore (90° included angle) to remove burrs.
13. The barrel shall be straightened to meet the requirements of optical straightness gage.
14. The operating rod assembly shall function, of its own weight, freely, and without binding during a simulated firing cycle with the operating rod spring removed.
15. The trigger pull required to release the hammer shall be smooth, free from "creep", and within the limits of four and one-half to six pounds. Functional surfaces of hammer, trigger and sear may have their phosphate coating removed by polishing.
16. Aperture assemblies 1005-864-2926 & 1005-8642928 produce 1/2 minute change of elevation by 180 degrees rotation of the aperture. Aperture assembly (standard) shall have an eyepiece with an 0.0595 peep hole. Aperture assembly (alternate) shall have an eyepiece with an 0.0520 peep hole.
17. Threads on windage knob and rear sight base shall be 5/16 - 64 NS-3 to produce 1/2 minute changes in windage. Elevation and windage knobs shall have free movement independent of each other, with definite clicking action and positive retention. Elevation knob must be at 100 meter setting when elevated 8 clicks from lowest position.
18. Top of front sight blade shall be square with side and all edges and corners shall be sharp to 0.003 R. Max. Front sight shall be sharp and square and shall not overhang the sides of the gas cylinder.
19. The flash suppressor shall be fastened securely to the barrel by the flash suppressor nut which in turn shall be fastened securely by a set screw. There shall be no rotational or longitudinal movement when examined manually. After assembly, a two diameter concentric plug shall be inserted in the muzzle of the flash suppressor and shall enter the barrel a minimum of 2.5 inches without binding in the flash suppressor.
20. The selector shaft, sear release, selector lock, and receiver sear release lug are permanently welded to eliminate full automatic capability.
21. Headspace, with component bolt, shall be from 1.6355 to 1.6385.
22. National Match identification marks for a complete rifle shall consist of the letters "NM" following rifle identification on the receiver, and the letters "NM" approximately 1/8 inch high inscribed on the barrel approximately midway between the front hand guard and front sight.

National Match Sights

1. The two aperture assemblies are identical except for the eyepieces which have different peep hole diameters. The aperture with 0.0595 peep hole will be installed as standard with the 0.0520 diameter aperture available as an alternate.

2. The hooded eyepiece is designed to eliminate glare and reflections on the sight aperture, and to provide 1/2 minute changes in elevation.

3. Each eyepiece is selectively fitted and matched with its individual aperture. It should not be disassembled to change the aperture assembly or to change eyepieces on the aperture. Each aperture assembly is selectively fitted and matched to the rear sight base.

4. The peep hole is 0.002" vertically eccentric with other diameters of the eyepiece. Rotating the eyepiece 180° clockwise or counter-clockwise raises and lowers the line of sight. Two spring loaded balls in the eyepiece engage a vertical "V" notch in the face of the aperture to retain the eyepiece in each position. The position of the eyepiece is indicated by a notch at the rear face of the eyepiece.

5. Each click of the elevation knob on the standard M14 rear sight gives a change of 1 minute of angle. Each click of the elevation knob on the National Match rear sight provides a change of 1/2 minute of angle. Rotating the eyepiece of the National Match aperture so that the indicator notch is at the top, moves the point of impact of the bullet up 1/2 minute. Rotating the indicator notch to the bottom, moves the point of impact down 1/2 minute, see Table B-1.

6. The National match sight base marked NM/2A is undercut to accept the hooded eyepiece. The change from 32 to 64 threads per inch in this sight base and of the windage knob are responsible for the ability to produce a 1/2 minute of change in windage for each click of either knob. Thus the 1967 National Match rifle is capable of 1/2 minute sight changes for both windage and elevation.

7. The National match front sight has a blade width of 0.065 -0. 005, and is identified by the letters "NM" and the numbers "062" on its right side.

Table B1 One Minute of Angle Change by Distance (For 1/2 minute of angle change, divde by 2)			
Yards		Meters	
Distance	Change (Inches)	Distance	Change (centimeters)
100	1.048	100	2.91
200	2.095	200	5.82
300	3.143	300	8.73
400	4.191	400	11.64
500	5.238	500	14.55
600	6.258	600	17.46
700	7.332	700	20.37
800	8.381	800	23.28
900	9.428	900	26.19
100	10.476	1000	29.10

APPENDIX C
DISASSEMBLY/REASSEMBLY OF THE M14-TYPE RIFLE

An overall exploded view of the M14-type rifle is shown in Figure C-1. Follow the instructions below for the proper disassembly/assembly sequence.

Fig. C-1. The M14-type rifle field stripped.

1.   Remove the magazine by depressing the magazine latch under the stock and ahead of the trigger guard. Push the latch forward and with your left hand, pull the back of the magazine down and forward, then ease it from the magazine well (Figure C-2).

Fig. C-2.

2.   Draw back the bolt handle and look inside to make certain the magazine and breech are empty. Depress the bolt lock and ease the bolt forward by keeping the edge of your right

hand on the operating rod handle. Push the safety to the on position (Figure C-3).

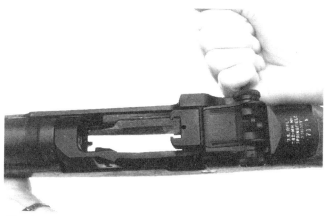

Fig. C-3.

3.   Turn the rifle upside down and rest the muzzle on a non-marring surface. Grasp the back of the trigger guard with the thumb and forefinger of the right hand and pull back and up. The trigger guard will unlatch. Draw the trigger assembly straight out of its recess (Figure C-4).

Fig. C-4.

4.   Rest your left hand on the rear sight assembly and grasp the sides of the receiver with your fingers. Lift up on the butt end of the stock with your right hand. The stock should separate from the barrel receiver. If it does not, gently tap the muzzle on the non-marring surface until the receiver loosens (Figure C-5).

Fig. C-5.

Note: If the receiver has been bedded in the stock, turn the rifle upside down. Rest the stock wrist and barrel on a padded block of wood. Lay another block of wood in the magazine well and with a hammer tap the receiver out of the bedded action.

5.   Lay the barreled action upside down. Press the end of the operating rod spring guide forward and at the same time with your finger nail or a metal shim on the protruding pin, move the operating guide pin to the left, relieving the tension of the operating rod spring. Lift the operating rod spring up and out of the operating rod (Figure C-6).

Fig. C-7.

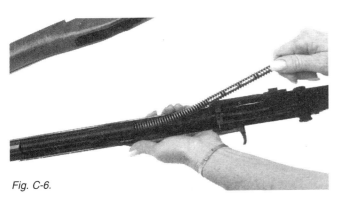

Fig. C-6.

Fig. C-8.

6.   Turn the barreled action upright. Draw the operating rod to the rear. M14 military rifles have a square cut in the guide rail on the right side while the commercial M14-type rifles have a semicircular cut in the rail similar to the M1 Garand. (Figure C-7). Draw the operating rod lug to this point and pull outward. The operating rod guide lug will leave the track and enable you to draw the operating rod out of its guide and away from the bolt roller (Figure C-8). If the fit is tight, tap it out with a brass hammer.

7.   With your fingers, pull the bolt back. Lifting and turning counterclockwise at the same time. This movement allows the rear of the bolt and the tail of the firing pin to clear the receiver (Figure C-9).

8.   Pry the handguard clips from their slots in the rear sides of the barrel and lift up and pull back and out (Figure C-10).

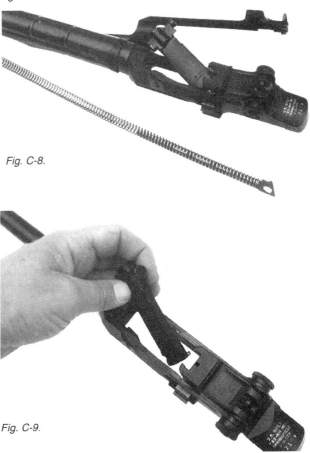

Fig. C-9.

9.   Use the combination tool to loosen the gas plug, then turn out. Unscrew the gas cylinder lock and move forward on the barrel out of the way. Place your hand in front of the gas cylinder and tip the barrel down. The gas piston will slide forward (Figure C-11).

11.   To disassemble the stock group remove the butt plate by taking out the top and bottom screws. Withdrawing the long lower buttplate screw will also free the rear swivel which can

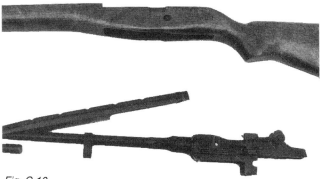

Fig. C-10.

be pulled down and out of the stock (Figure C-12).

Fig. C-11.

This completes the field stripping process. To reassemble, reverse the steps described above.

To detail strip the rifle, complete the following steps. Detail stripping should be done sparingly to prevent wear and tear on the parts.

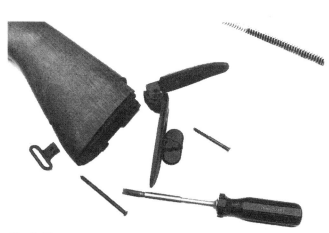

Fig. C-12.

12. To remove the flashhider/front sight assembly, use the flash suppressor pliers to unscrew the round, knurled nut (Castle nut), grasp the flashhider and unscrew. Separate the nut from the flashhider.

13. To remove the front sight, unscrew the set screw at the rear. **Note**: first scribe a line on the front sight base and the flashhider base to assist in recentering.

14. To remove the bolt release from the left side of the receiver, use a drift punch to remove the roll pin holding it in place.

15. To remove the stock liners, use the proper size spanner and remove the screws holding them in place.

16. To disassemble the bolt, it is best to have an M1/M14 bolt disassembly tool. Move the handle to the forward position and place the bolt into the channel so that the ejector is opposite the ejector stud in the tool. Press the handle forward as far as it will go (Figure C-13).

18). Depress the stud on the bottom of the tool to raise the extractor from its recess. Lay the extractor aside. Ease the handle to the rear and lift the bolt from the channel. Tip back to allow the firing pin to slide out. To remove the extractor spring, carefully pry it from its recess with a small-bladed screwdriver or knife point (Figure C-14).

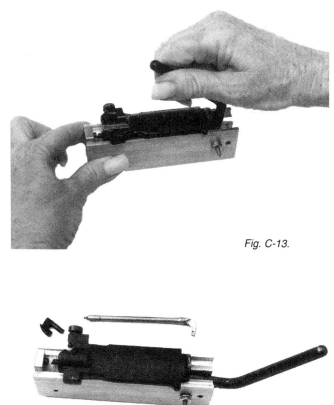

Fig. C-13.

Fig. C-14.

17. If you do not have a bolt removal tool, the bolt can still be be disassembled as follows. Hold in your left hand with the face of the bolt up and the operating lug to the right. Place your little finger under the firing pin tang and your thumb over the ejector. The ejector spring is under compression and may fly out if you don't. Insert a thin-bladed screwdriver between the extractor and the lower cartridge flange and pry the extractor up and out of its seat. Release your thumb pressure carefully and remove the ejector and spring.

18. To reassemble, reverse with the process.

19. When disassembling the trigger assembly, it should be latched closed. Pull the trigger and ease the hammer forward. Hold the assembly in the palm of either hand with the trigger guard to the right and your thumb over the hammer. Place your index and middle fingers over the back of the sear and the press against sear and trigger. Use a bullet tip or a punch to drift out the trigger pin. Release tension on the hammer spring.

20. Lift out the trigger and sear assembly, then remove the hammer spring housing, spring and hammer spring plunger.

21. Drift out the hammer pin. Rotate the hammer to the rear and remove it. Open the trigger guard. Drift out the safety stud and remove the safety.

22. To remove the trigger guard, grasp the rear of the trigger guard with the right hand, swing it down and draw it to the rear until the holes in the wings are aligned with the safety stud hole. At this point the hammer stop will clear the base. Swing the trigger guard to the right and upward, removing it. You may have to vary the position slightly to wriggle it free.

23. To reassemble the trigger assembly, hold the trigger housing at the rearmost portion with the left hand, vertical face to the front, open side to the right. Grasp the trigger guard at the latch end, and place the wings astride the base of the trigger housing at the same point from which the trigger guard was removed. Swing the trigger guard down and to the left, then slide it forward into position.

24. Replace the safety by inserting the finger piece through its slot in the base of the housing, and seat the safety stud in its hole in the side of the housing. In seating the safety, some downward pressure against the short arm of the clip ejector is necessary. Push the finger piece to its forward position. Swing the trigger guard to its open position and replace the hammer in a half-cocked position, making sure that the toe is in front of the hammer stop. Align the holes in the hammer, the housing, and the wings of the trigger guard and insert the hammer pin, oscillating the trigger guard and hammer, seating the pin fully. Do not force it.

25. Assemble the hammer-spring housing, hammer spring, and hammer spring plunger into one unit. Place the trigger housing on the table, open side to your front, vertical face to left, hammer up. Place the nose of the plunger in its seat on the hammer, being sure that the cutaway portion of the hammer-spring housing is toward the safety. With the palm of the left hand over the hammer hold the hammer spring housing, hammer spring, and hammer-spring plunger in place with the fingers of the left hand.

26. Insert the finger piece of the trigger through the trigger slot, so that the notch is above the base of the housing. Allow the wings of the hammer-spring housing to straddle the sear pin. When properly placed you can see the ends of the sear pin through the holes in the wings. Press back on the finger piece of the trigger with the right forefinger, and push on the sear with the right thumb. Steady the hammer-spring housing with the left fingers. Press down quickly on the sear, align the holes for the trigger pin, and insert the trigger pin to its head only.

27. To seat the head of the trigger pin, turn your right hand palm up and grasp the trigger group so that the top of the hammer is toward the body and the open side is up, the right thumb in rear of the sear, the first and second fingers grasping the vertical face. Apply a sudden squeeze by strongly attempting to close the right hand and at the same time seat the trigger pin by applying pressure on its head with the left thumb.

APPENDIX D
ACCURACY MEASUREMENT

EXCERPTED FROM "1967 NATIONAL MATCH RIFLES," U.S. ARMY MATERIAL COMMAND.

The object of shooting a rifle or pistol is to hit something. We can rate a weapon, then, based on your ability to make high scores with it, but this rating method is not satisfactory, as it includes personal ability, weather conditions and many other factors. In order to compare ammunition or weapon-ammunition combinations they are fired under conditions eliminating as much as possible of the human and weather error, and the resulting groupings of shots on the target are measured and compared. But there are various methods of measuring the shot groups — each method having certain advantages. Some of these will be discussed.

Extreme spread (ES) is the easy choice, as it involves only a quick estimate by eye and one measurement. As it infers, you merely measure between the widest two shots of the group, regardless of whether the measurement is vertical, horizontal or in-between. It is a useful sort of measure for the target shooter, who is interested in getting all of his shots in a certain small-sized bull's-eye.

Maximum spread does not give you any information on the shape of the group, i.e., whether it is strung up and down, wide laterally or symmetrical in shape.

A couple more measurements will readily give you this information. By getting the vertical distance between the top and the bottom shots of the group you will have the *extreme vertical* (EV). The horizontal distance between the left and the right shots of the group will give you the *extreme horizontal* (EH). Extreme vertical and extreme horizontal are frequently less than the extreme spread, may be equal to it, but cannot be larger than the extreme spread. See Figure D-1.

A puffy, lateral wind tends to spread a group side ways and this effect may overshadow the normal lateral dispersion. You may want to forget about extreme horizontal spread for this reason, or you may want to compare different cartridges shot under the same sort of conditions for both accuracy and sensitivity to wind by using figure of merit as your yardstick.

Figure of merit (F/M) as used in the USA, is the sum of the extreme vertical plus the extreme horizontal, divided by two. While figure of merit isn't used too often, you sometimes run into it, particularly in connection with the .22 rifle.

Before going further, we should discuss the point from which you measure, that is, whether from the inside, center or outside edge of the bullet holes. It is customary to measure from center to center of bullet holes, rather than from inside or outside edge. If there is any doubt, the point of measurement should be specified.

As you can readily see, extreme measurements give a great deal of importance to a single shot. To rescue this distorted value given to a single shot, in military ammunition it is customary to use the *mean radius* (MR) as the accuracy measure. Mean radius is more trouble to get, but it provides information not given by the simpler extreme measurements.

A rough-and-ready way of getting the center of impact is to draw a vertical line with the same number of shots on each side of the line and approximately dividing the distance between the two innermost shots. Fire ten shots at a target. Draw a horizontal line in the same fashion. The point where these two lines cross is pretty close to the *center of impact* (C/I) close enough for sight changes, although not good enough for the next step in getting the mean radius.

From the accurate center of impact you measure the distance to each of the shot holes, as shown in Figure D-2. Add these figures, divide by 10 and there it is — the mean radius!

An approximation of the mean radius can be obtained by adding the extreme vertical and the extreme horizontal measurements and dividing by five, or if you want to get some idea of extreme spread, multiply the mean radius by three. Don't trust these approximate methods too far as they can be way off on occasions.

Since mean radius is the result of an averaging process, it's possible for extreme spread to vary considerably in different groups that have the same mean radius. While this is an extreme case, it is something to consider when you're thinking about mean radius.

Closely related to mean radius are mean vertical deviation and mean horizontal deviation. To get mean vertical deviation, measure vertically from the horizontal line through the center of impact to each shot, total these measurements and divide by 10. Mean horizontal deviation is similarly measured, but horizontally from the vertical line through the center of impact. Since these also are averaging measurements, they are subject to the same difficulties as mean radius, but do tell you whether the error is mainly vertical or horizontal. As with the measurements of extremes, mean vertical and mean horizontal deviations can't be greater than the mean radius.

While there are many other methods of measuring or expressing accuracy — probable error, standard deviations, variance, etc. — the methods outlined here are most satisfactory in small arms, target shooting field.

The accuracy with which the distances should be measured depend on the group size, equipment available, and the accuracy required. To get measurements accurate to about 1%, means that small group (around 1-2 inches) should be measured to the nearest hundredth inch (.01), moderate sized group (around 10 inches to the nearest tenth inch (.1) and larger groups to the nearest half inch or inch. An average should be given in the same figures as the individual measurements.

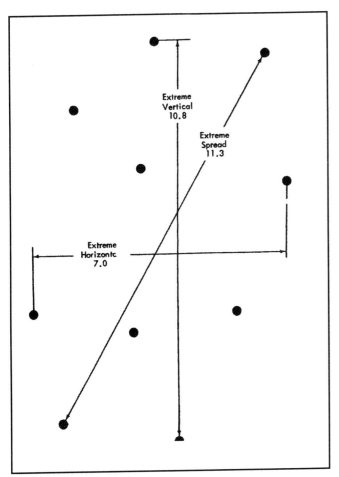

Fig. D-1.

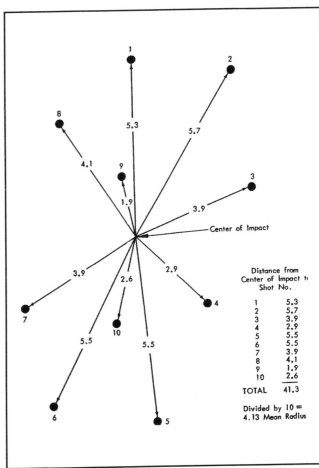

Fig. D-2.

Accurizing Cryo, Division of 300° Below, Inc. 1160 S. Monroe, Decatur, IL 62521. Computer controlled cryogenic accurizing of rifle barrels.

Amtreat Cryogenics, 24374 Clipstone St., Woodland Hills, CA 91367 818 888-8664. Computer-controlled cyrogenic rifle barrel tempering.

Armory of Orange, 368 South Tustin, Orange, CA 92666, 714 532-4233, parts, accessories, M14 tools and gages.

Armscorp USA, Inc., 4424 John Avenue, Baltimore, MD 21227. 410 247-6200, FAX 410 247-6205. M14 semiautomatic rifles and investment cast receivers, T48 semiautomatic rifles and receivers, parts and accessories.

Berger Bullets, Ltd., 5342 West Camelback Rd., Ste 200, Glendale, AZ 85301. 602 842-4001. FAX 602 934-9083, Website: bergerbullets@bergerbullet.com.

Black Hills Ammunition, Inc., PO Box 3090, Rapid City, SD 57709-3090. 605 348-5150, FAX 605 348-9827.

B. Jones Lens Systems, 5115 E. Edgemont, Phoenix AZ 85008. 602 840-2176. Website: http://bjonessights.com; Email:bjones-sights@uswestmail.com

Brownells, Inc. Rte 2, Box 1, Montezuma, IA 50171. 515 623-5401. Gunsmithing tools, jigs and aids, M14 barrels, stocks and parts. Indispensable.

Century Arms International, 48 Lower Newton, St. Albans, VT 05478 802 527-1252 (Parts Kits)

Champion's Choice, Inc., 201 International Blvd., La Vergne, TN 37086. 615 793-4066, FAX 793-4070. Scoring books, wide assortment of shooting accessories.

Civilian Marksmanship Program, PO Box 576, Port Clinton, OH 43452. Email: custserv@odcmp.com; web site: http://www.odcmp.com. The DCM has selected M14 and M1 Garand parts available. You must be a member of the NRA and a local DCM-affiliated club (virtually all state rifle and pistol associations) and request an official order form from the above address. You may order two of any available parts.

Creedmore Sports, Inc., PO Box 1040, Oceanside, CA 92051, Order desk 800 273-3366, Inquiries 619 757-5529, FAX 757-5558. Precision and Match rifles, books, videos, and shooting supplies.

Cryogenic Tempering /-300, PO Box 404 Center & Market Streets, Seville, OH 216 769-1495, FAX 216 769-1496. Cryogenic rifle barrel tempering.

Dillon Precision Products, Inc., 8009 E Dillon's Way, Scottsdale, AZ 85260 800 223-4570, FAX 602 998-2786. A range of shooting supplies and reloading equipment.

Douglas Barrels, Inc., 5504 Big Tyler Rd., Charleston, WV 25313, 304 776-1341 FAX 304 776-8560, Website:

Entréprise Arms, 15861 Business Center, Irwindale, CA 91706. 626 962-8712, 626 962-4692 (Fax) Internet: www.entreprise.com. Manufacturer of exceptionally well-made, machined M14A2 semiautomatic receivers, and the Tactical 2 M141A/M21 Mount Foundation, one of the finest telescopic sight mounting systems for the M14/M14-type rifle. Also manufactures CNC-machined L1A1 and FAL upper receivers in inch and Israeli patterns and supplies metric upper receivers.

Federal Cartridge Company, 900 Ellen Drive, Anoka MN 55303. 612 323-2300.

Fulton Armory, 8725 Bolman Place, Savage, MD 20763. 301 490-9485 U.S. military gun parts.

Gun Parts Corporation, West Hurley, NY 12491. U.S. military gun parts of all kinds.

Harris Rifle Company, 3840 N 28th Ave, Phoenix, AZ 85017 Excellent, hand-laid fiberglass stocks. 602 582-9627 FAX 602 230-1422

Hart Rifle Barrels, Inc., P.O. Box 182, 1690 Apulia Road, LaFayette, NY 13084. 315 677-9841 FAX 315 677-9610, Website: www.hartbarrels.com.

Hornady Match Bullets and Ammo, PO Box 1848, Grand Island, NE 68802-1848. Website: www.hornady.com.

H-S Precision, Inc., 1301 Turbine Drive, Rapid City , South Dakota 57703. 605 341 - 3006, FAX 605 342 - 8964, Website: hsprecision.com.

Krieger Barrels, Inc., North 114 West 18697 Clinton Drive, Germantown , Wisconsin 53022, 262 255 - 9593, FAX 262 255 - 9586, Website: Kreigerbarrels.com.

M14 Research Service, 7476 132nd Way North, Seminole, FL 34646. Ordnance drawings and prints, original and reproduction, tools, gauges and parts.

MacMillan Fiberglass Stocks, Inc., 21421 N. 14th Avenue, Phoenix, AZ 85027, 602 582-9635.

Obermeyer Rifle Barrels, Inc., 23122 60th St, Bristol, WI 53102, 414 843-3537, FAX 414 843-2129.

Placer CBS, 3945 Grass Valley Hwy, #47, Auburn, CA 95602 916 885-6892 (Parts)

RSI, 25132 Ridge Rd, Colona, IL 61241 309 441-6253 (FAX) 441-6256 (Parts kits, parts and supplies)

Rock Island Armory, 25144 Ridge Road, Colona, IL 61241. Complete M14 U.S. GI parts kits — everything but the receiver. Also specializes in M14 stocks and other parts. This is a private company, not the national arsenal.

Shilen Rifle Barrels, Inc., 12202 N 62nd Place, Scottsdale, AZ 85254. 602-948-2525.

Smith Enterprises 1701 W 10th St, Tempe AZ 85281. Service grade, single and double-lugged, precision investment cast M14-type receivers. Also heat treatment services for Chinese-made M14 rifles. 480 964-1818 FAX 921-9987 Internet www.smithenterprise.com

Springfield Armory, Springfield Inc., 420 West Main St., Geneseo, IL 61254. The largest manufacturer of commercial M14 rifles, under the trade marked name, M1A. Also parts and customizing. This is a private company, not the national arsenal. 309 944-5631, Fax 309 944-3676. Email Spring@Geneseo.net. Internet web site www.springfield-armory.com.

SARCO, Inc., 323 Union Street, Stirling, NJ 07980. A major supplier of parts for the M14 and other U.S. military firearms.

William J. Ricca Surplus Sales, PO Box 25, New Tripoli, PA 18066. 610 298-2748, FAX 610 298-2540. Maintains a wide inventory of M14 and other U.S. military rifle parts. Also accessories and scope mounts.

M14 Gunsmithing Services

Armscorp USA, Inc., 4424 John Avenue, Baltimore, MD 21227. 410 247-6200, FAX 410 247-6205.

Capalbo, John, Garden Grove, CA., Phone 714 539-5552. Custom gunsmithing, M14-type semiautomatic rifles assembled.

Evan's Gunsmithing's Shooter's World, 1935 N. Enterprise, Orange CA 92865 714 283-5248.

Grúning Precision, 7101 Jurupa Ave., Ste 12 Riverside, CA 92500. Contact **Jim Gronning** 909 689-6692, FAX 909 689-7791. Email: Gruningprecision@earthlink.net. Custom built high power match rifles, full range gunsmithing services. Specializing in M14-type, M1 Garand and bolt action precision rifles for civilian and military match shooters and sniper rifles for law enforcement and the military.

Clint Fowler Rifles, Custom Gunsmithing, 10486 Stegara Road, Barboursville, VA 22923. Phone 540 672-0357. Custom built M14-type and M1 Garand match rifles and services.

Entréprise Arms, 16021 E. Arrow Highway, Unit B, Irwindale, CA 91706. 818 962-8712, FAX 818 962-4692. CNC machined M14-type semiautomatic receivers, M14-type scope mounts and sights.

Fred Johnson, National Armorer, 5037 N 54th Ave., #1, Glendale, AZ 85301, 602 435-8279. Custom built high power match rifles, custom stocks.

Tim La France, P.O. Box 178211, San Diego 92177 CA 619 293-3373 FAX 619 297-0577. Custom built high power match rifles, custom building services.

S.A.W. (Ken Elmore), 14615 S 41st Place, Phoenix AZ 85044.

APPENDIX F
THE LEGAL RAMIFICATIONS OF BUILDING SEMIAUTOMATIC RIFLES

The Bureau of Alcohol, Tobacco and Firearms has recently clarified federal firearms regulations regarding the assembly from parts kits of semiautomatic rifles which are banned from federal *importation* or manufacture under the provisions of the 1994 Violent Crime Act.

Domestic Semiautomatic Firearms Banned From Manufacture

The 1994 "Violent Crime Act" restricts the manufacture of domestically produced semiautomatic rifles. You are no longer allowed to assemble such a rifle if it includes two or more of the following "banned" items: folding or telescopic stock, pistol grip, bayonet mount, flash suppressor (flashhider) or threaded barrel (at the muzzle) and a grenade launcher. Also, any detachable magazine with a capacity greater than 10 rounds cannot be used.

In short, the law now prevents you from purchasing a "parts kit" and assembling it, or having it assembled to a receiver, either original, reproduction or replacement, whether manufactured in this country or a foreign country, if the completed firearm is identical to the original proscribed rifle or uses more than ten imported parts if manufactured abroad.

In the case of the M14 which as originally built has neither a folding stock or telescopic sight or pistol grip but did have a bayonet mount, flashhider and threaded barrel, to conform to provisions of the 1994 Violent Crime Act, you could remove the flash suppressor and substitute a muzzle brake, and cut off the bayonet mount. You can also substitute a newly-manufactured ten round magazine and, of course, refrain from mounting a grenade launcher.

Imported Semiautomatic Firearms

Paragraph 178.39 of Section 27 of the Code of Federal Regulations states that no one can assemble a semiautomatic rifle or any shotgun using more than ten *imported* parts. The BATF lists twenty parts of which no more than ten can be used: 1) frames, receivers, receiver castings, forgings or stampings, 2) barrels, 3) barrel extensions, 4) mounting blocks (trunnions), 5) muzzle attachments, 6) bolts, 7) bolt carriers, 8) operating rods) 9) gas pistons, 10) trigger housings, 11) triggers, 12) hammers, 13) sears, 14) disconnectors, 15) buttstocks, 16) pistol grips, 17) forearms or handguard, 18) magazine bodies, 19) followers, 20) floorplates. The only exceptions allowed to this rule are the assembly of rifles for sale or distribution to a governmental body, or for testing or experimentation with the permission of the BATF, *or the repair of, or the replacement of* any part on a now-banned rifle or shotgun that was imported into the United States *prior* to November 30, 1990. It was on this date that President George Bush issued an executive order banning the importation or manufacture of "assault rifles."

The semiautomatic firearms currently listed as "assault rifles" included all models of or copies of the Norinco, Polytech or Mitchell AK47, UZI, Galil, Beretta AR70 (SC70), Colt AR-15, FAL, FNC, MAC 10,11 or 12, Steyr AUG, INTRATEC TEC-9 and variations; all variations of the Striker, Street Sweeper or USAS 12 shotgun. The current ban further includes any semiautomatic rifle that can accept a detachable magazine and has at least two of the following parts: folding or telescopic stock, pistol grip, bayonet mount, flash suppressor or threaded barrel and grenade launcher. The ban further includes any pistol with any of the above parts plus a barrel shroud and which weighs 50 ounces or more, unloaded. Also any semiautomatic shotgun that has any of the above parts plus a fixed magazine capacity in excess of five rounds, or a detachable magazine.

Canfield, Bruce, "Winchester in Service," Andrew Mowbray, Inc., Lincoln, RI 02865.

Duff, Scott A., "The M1 Garand: Owner's Guide," Scott Duff Publications, Export, PA 15632, 1994.

Duff, Scott A., and John M. Miller, "The M14 Owner's Guide and Match Conditioning Instructions," Scott Duff Publications, Export, PA 15632, 1996.

Ezell, Edward Clinton, "The Great Rifle Controversy," Stackpole Books, Harrisburg, PA 17105 1984.

Faatz, Wayne, "The Mysterious Slam Fire," *American Rifleman*, 11250 Waples Mill Road, Fairfax VA 22030, Phone 800 336-7402. October 1953.

_____, "Federal Firearms Regulations Reference Guide," Department of the Treasury, Bureau of Alcohol, Tobacco and Firearms," ATF P 5300.4 (10-95), U.S. Government Printing Office, Washington DC, 20402-9328, 1995.

Hatcher, Julian S., "Hatcher's Notebook," Stackpole Books, Harrisburg, PA 1947, rev. ed. 1966.

Kuhnhausen, Jerry, "The U.S. .30 Caliber Gas Operated Service Rifles, A Shop Manual, Volumes I and II," Heritage-VSP Gun Books, Box 887, McCall ID 83638, 1995, Phone 208 634-4104. Fax 208 634-3101.

McNaugher, Thomas L., "Marksmanship, McNamara and the M16 Rifle: Organizations, Analysis and Weapons Acquisitions," Delivered at the March 21-24, 1979 International Studies Association, Toronto, Ontario. From the Rand Corporation Collection.

____, "NRA High Power Rifle Rules," National Rifle Association of America, 11250 Waples Mill Road, Fairfax VA 22030, 1997, Phone 800 336-7402.

Pullum, Bill and Frank T. Hanenkrat, "Position Rifle Shooting," Privately Printed, Available through the National Rifle Association, 11250 Waples Mill Road, Fairfax, VA 22030-9400, 1985, Phone 703 267-1600.

Senich, Peter R., The Complete Book of U.S. Sniping," Paladin Press, Boulder, CO 80306, 1988.

Senich, Peter R., The Long Range War — Sniping in Vietnam," Paladin Press, Boulder, CO 80306, 1994.

Sloan, E.F., Col., USA ret'd., "Champion National Match Course Score Book," Champion's Choice, Inc., Nashville, TN 37211, 1972.

Stephen, Lewis, "The M14 and its Civilian Counterpart, the M1A," *Banned Guns 2*, Challenge Publications, Canoga Park, CA 91304, 1995.

Stevens, R. Blake, "U.S. Rifle M14, from John Garand to the M21," Collector Grade Publications, PO Box 250, Station E, Toronto, ONT M6H 4E2, 1983.

___, "The M1 Rifle," American Rifleman Reprint, National Rifle Association, 11250 Waples Mill Rd, Fairfax VA 22030-9400.

___, M-14 Rifle Accurization, Guide to National Match Accurizing as Performed by U.S. Army Shooting Team Gunsmiths, U.S. Army Marksmanship Unit, Fort Benning GA 31905.

___, 1967 National Match Rifles, U.S. Cal. 7.62 mm M14 and U.S. Cal. 30 M1 National Match Ammunition," U.S. Army Material Command, U.S. Army Weapons Command, U.S. Army Munition Command.

TM-9-1005-222-12, "Operator and Organizational Maintenance Manual Including Repair Parts and Special Tools List, Rifle Caliber .30: M1, W/E (1005-674-1425), Rifle, Caliber .30: M1C (Sniper's) W/E (1005-674-1430), Rifle, Caliber .30: M1D (Sniper's) W/E (1005-674-1431), Headquarters, Department of the Army, 1969.

TM9-1005-222-12P/1, "Operator and Organizational Maintenance Repair Parts and Special Tool Lists for Rifle 7.62 mm, M14 National Match and Rifle 7.62 mm, M14(m)," Headquarters, Department of the Army, Washington D.C., February 1968.

TM9-1005-223-12P, "Operator and Organizational Maintenance Repair Parts and Special Tool Lists for Caliber .30 U.S. Rifle M1 (National Match)," Headquarters, Department of the Army, Washington D.C.,1963.

TM 9-1005-223-20, "Organizational Maintenance Manual Including Repair Parts and Special Tool Lists for Rifle, 7.62 mm, M14, W/E/ (1005-589-1271); Rifle, 7.62 mm, M14A1, W/E/ (1005-072-5001); Bipod, Rifle M1 (1005-711-6202), Headquarters, Department of the Army, August 1972.

TM 9-1005-223-35, "Direct, Support, General Support, and Depot Maintenance Manual Including Repair Parts and Special Tools List: 7.62 mm, M14, W/E/ (1005-589-1271); Rifle, 7.62 mm, M14A1, W/E/ (1005-072-5001); Bipod, Rifle M1 (1005-711-6202)," Headquarters, Department of the Army, August 1968.

About the Author

Joe Poyer is the author of more than 400 magazine articles on firearms, the modern military, military history and personal security. He written and published twelve novels with worldwide sales exceeding five million copies and authored or co-authored nine non-fiction books on the modern military.

He is the owner and publisher of North Cape Publications which publishes the "For Collectors Only" series of books for firearms collectors. In this series, he has written or co-authored, "The .45-70 Springfield," "U.S. Winchester Trench and Riot Guns, and other U.S. Combat Shotguns," and "The M1 Garand 1936 to 1957" and the "SKS Carbine." "The M14-Type Rifles" is the first in a new series of books (For Shooters and Collectors Only) from North Cape.

Mr. Poyer has served as editor of the following magazines: *Safe & Secure Living*; *International Military Review*, *International Naval Review* and as field editor for *International Combat Arms*. He is currently at work on two new books in "The For Collectors Only" series; "The Colt Single Action: Four Generations" and the "Model 1917 Enfield" and a new book for in the "Shooters and Collectors Only" series, "FAL: Free World's Battle Rifle."

Mr. Poyer was the on-camera Military Affairs Analyst and Reporter for a major television station in Los Angeles, California. He also imported the very fine L1A1A inch pattern FAL rifles from Australia in the late 1980s.

Other Books from North Cape Publications®, Inc.

The books in the "For Collectors Only" series are designed to provide the firearm's collector with an accurate record of the markings, dimensions and finish found on an original firearm as it was shipped from the factory. As changes to any and all parts are listed by serial number range, the collector can quickly assess not only whether or not the overall firearm is correct as issued, but whether or not each and every part is original for the period of the particular firearm's production. "For Collectors Only" books make each collector an "expert."

The .45-70 Springfield by Joe Poyer and Craig Riesch ($16.95) covers the entire range of .45 caliber "trapdoor" Springfield arms, the gun that really won the west. "Virtually a mini-encyclopedia . . . this reference piece is a must." Phil Spangenberger, *Guns & Ammo*

U.S. Winchester Trench and Riot Guns and other U.S. Combat Shotguns by Joe Poyer ($15.95). Describes the elusive and little-known "Trench Shotgun" and all other combat shotguns used by U.S. military forces. "U.S. military models 97 and 12 Trench and Riot Guns, their parts, markings [and] dimensions [are examined] in great detail . . . a basic source of information for collectors." C.R. Suydam, *Gun Report*

The M1 Carbine: Wartime Production by Craig Riesch ($16.95) describes the four models of M1 Carbines from all ten manufacturers. Complete with codes for every part by serial number range. "The format makes it extremely easy to use. The book is a handy reference for beginning or experienced collectors." Bruce Canfield, Author of "M1 Garand and M1 Carbine"

The M1 Garand 1936 to 1957 by Joe Poyer and Craig Riesch ($19.95). "The book covers such important identification factors as manufacturer's markings, proof marks, final acceptance cartouches stampings, heat treatment lot numbers . . . there are detailed breakdowns of . . . every part . . . in minute detail. This 216 page . . . volume is easy to read and full of identification tables, parts diagrams and other crucial graphics that aid in determining the originality of your M1 and/or its component parts." Phil Spangenberger, *Guns and Ammo*

Winchester Lever Action Repeating Firearms, by Arthur Pirkle.
    Volume 1, **The Models of 1866, 1873 & 1876** ($19.95)
    Volume 2, **The Models of 1886 and 1892** ($19.95)
    Volume 3, **The Models of 1894 and 1895** ($19.95)
These famous lever action repeaters are completely analyzed part-by-part by serial number range in this first new book on these fine weapons in twenty years. ". . . book is truly for the serious collector . . . Mr. Pirkle's scholarship is excellent and

his presentation of the information . . . is to be commended." H.G.H., *Man at Arms*

The SKS Carbine, by Steve Kehaya and Joe Poyer ($16.95).The "SKS Carbine" is profusely illustrated, articulately researched and covers all aspects of its development as well as . . . other combat guns used by the USSR and other Communist bloc nations. Each component . . . from stock to bayonet lug, or lack thereof, is covered along with maintenance procedures . . . because of Kehaya's and Poyer's book, I have become the leading expert in West Texas on [the SKS].Glen Voorhees, Jr., *Gun Week*

British Enfield Rifles, by Charles R. Stratton
    Volume 1, **SMLE (No. 1) Mk I and Mk III** ($16.95)
"Stratton . . . does an admirable job of . . . making sense of . . . a seemingly hopeless array of marks and models and markings and apparently endless varieties of configurations and conversions . . . this is a book that any collector of SMLE rifles will want on his shelf." Alan Petrillo, *The Enfield Collector's Digest*

    Volume 2, **The Lee-Enfield No. 4 and No. 5 Rifles** ($16.95)
In Volume 2, "Skip" Stratton provides a concise but extremely thorough analysis of the famed British World War II rifle, the No. 4 Enfield, and the No. 5 Rifle, better known as the "Jungle Carbine." It's all here, markings, codes, parts, manufacturers and history of development and use.

The Mosin-Nagant Rifle by Terence W Lapin ($19.95). For some reason, in the more than 100 years that the Mosin-Nagant rifle has been in service around the world, not a single book has been written in English about this fine rifle. Now, just as interest in the Mosin-Nagant is exploding, Terence W. Lapin had written a comprehensive volume that covers all aspects and models from the Imperial Russian rifles to the Finnish, American, Polish, Chinese, Romanian and North Korean variations. His books set a standard that future authors will find very difficult to best.

M14-Type Rifles, A Shooter's and Collector's Guide, by Joe Poyer ($14.95). A study of the U.S. Army's last and shortest-lived .30 caliber battle rifle which became a popular military sniper and civilian high power match rifle. A detailed look at the National Match M14 rifle, the M21 sniper rifle and the currently-available civilian semiautomatic match rifles, receivers, parts and accessories, including the Chinese M14s. A guide to custom-building a service type-rifle or a match grade, precision rifle. Includes a list of manufacturers and parts suppliers, plus the BATF regulations for building a "banned" rifle look-alike.

The SAFN-49 Battle Rifle, A Shooter's and Collector's Guide, by Joe Poyer ($14.95). The SAFN-49, the predecessor of the Free World's battle rifle, the FAL, has long been neglected by arms historians and writers, but not by collectors. Developed in the 1930s at the same time as the M1 Garand and the SVT38/40, the SAFN-49 did not reach production because of the Nazi invasion of Belgium until after World War II. This study of the SAFN-49 provides a part-by-part examination of the four calibers in which the rifle was made. Also, a thorough discussion of the SAFN-49 Sniper Rifle plus maintenance, assembly/disassembly, accurizing, restoration and shooting. A new exploded view and section view are included.

The Swedish Mauser Rifles by Steve Kehaya and Joe Poyer ($19.95). The first book in English and the most complete ever written on these fine military firearms. Built with all the craftsmanship and precision of a Volvo, the Swedish Mauser and its 6.5 x 55 mm cartridge have long been considered the finest combination of military rifle and ammunition ever developed. The Swedish Mauser is known for its amazing accuracy and durability. Kehaya and Poyer have produced a most thorough history of its development and use by Swedish military forces during the late 19th and throughout the 20th century; a survey of all fourteen variations of the three major models; a part-by-part analysis to assist the collector in determining the authenticity of his or her rifle; a complete discussion of all sniper rifle models; a description of all accessories issued to the soldier; ammunition; disassembly/assembly and a discussion of production methods and totals and a serial number list developed from an extensive data base of serial numbers by model.

Campaign Clothing: Field Uniforms of the Indian War Army
>**Volume 1, 1866 to 1871 ($12.95)**
>**Volume 2, 1872 to 1886 ($14.95)**
Lee A. Rutledge has produced a unique perspective on the uniforms of the Army of the United States during the late Indian War period following the Civil War. He discusses what the soldier really wore when on campaign. No white hats and yellow bandanas here.

A Guide Book to U.S. Army Dress Helmets 1872-1904, by Mark Kasal and Don Moore ($16.95).
From 1872 to 1904, the men and officer's of the U.S. Army wore a fancy, plumed or spiked helmet on all dress occassions. As ubiquitous as they were in the late 19th Century, they are extremely scarce today. Kasal and Moore have written a step-by-step, part-by-part analysis of both the Model 1872 and 1881 dress helmets and their history and use. Profusely illustrated with black and white and color photographs of actual helmets.

All of the above books can be obtained directly from North Cape Publications®, Inc, P.O. Box 1027, Tustin, CA 92781 or by calling Toll Free 1-800 745-9714. Orders only to the toll free number please. For information, call 714 832-3621. Orders may also be placed by FAX (714 832-5302) or via Email to ncape@pacbell.net. CA residents add 7.75% sales tax. Postage is currently $2.75 for 1-2 books, $3.25 for 3-4 books, $4.95 for 5-8 books. Call for postage on quantities for 9 books and more.

Also, visit our Internet web site at **http://www.north-capepubs.com**. Our complete, up-to-date book list can always be found there. Also check out our linked On-Line Magazine for the latest in firearms-related, magazine-quality articles and excerpts from our books.

M14 Notes

M14 Notes

M14 Notes

M14 Notes